A Guide for Republican Candidates

This Book Promotes the Traditional GOP Principles of 'Limited Government', and 'Comply with the Constitution'. This Approach ALWAYS Gives More Liberty, Peace, and Prosperity.

By: David Redick

Edition	Issue Date	Pages
First	April 15, 2017	186

Published by 'Forward USA Foundation' (Forward-USA.org)

Library of Congress: ISBN-13: 978-1545412039 , ISBN-10: 1545412030

Printed in the USA by CreateSpace.com, a DBA of On-Demand Publishing LLC, part of the Amazon group of companies.

This book is available at a leading on-line shopping service. Other books by Dave are there also.

Dedication

In any free market, capitalistic democracy, it is a constant battle to prevent self-serving, greedy people, (including Oligarchs, Neoconservatives, Socialists, Progressives, Liberals, and Communists), from gaining control of the government. History and logic show us that their methods **ALWAYS** lead to less peace and economic productivity, and more war and welfare.

This book is offers ideas and info sources to help the concerned and government-active citizens of the USA, who support the GOP principles shown herein, and seek office in order to monitor, and correct any unconstitutional, or counterproductive policies, and actions of people involved in government decision making and influence. They will submit bills to implement their ideas, and terminate bad laws and policies! These '**Limited Government' activists** are usually about 5% of the population **(the Shepherds to Guard and Guide the Herd)**, with 60% inactive **(the Sheep)**, and 35% '**Big Government' activists (the Wolves)** seeking benefits (subsidies, legal favors, etc.) for themselves or their employer.

We extend the 5% a big; **Thank You!**

This book will be active 'forever', and will be updated as events require in the months and years ahead.

Please send your questions or suggestions to Dave at RedickD@AOL.com.

Wise Words

"Government is not reason; it is not eloquence; it is force. Like fire, it is a dangerous servant and a fearful master." George Washington

"Government is not a solution to our problems, it is the problem"; Ronald Reagan spoke these words at his first inauguration on Jan. 20, 1981

Paul Craig Roberts, PhD. (PaulCraigRoberts.org) wrote; "Washington's argument is that unless Americans accept the most complete police-state in history, they will not be safe. Consequently, today no American is safe from his own government."

Richard Ebeling, PhD. (rebeling@citadel.edu), Sep-2015; 'Critics of capitalism constantly insist on the "failure" of the free market, from the news pundits to the leftist leaders of political parties. Yet, in fact, the asserted "failures" of capitalism are really the inevitable results of the interventionist-welfare state, and the close relationships between government and special interest groups popularly called "crony capitalism'.

Sen. Jack Kemp said; "1. There are no limits to our future if we don't put limits on our people, 2. It is empirically true and historically convincing that with lower rates of taxation on labor, capital, and the factors of production, you will get a bigger economy.";

"The only thing necessary for the triumph of evil is for good people to do nothing.", Edmund Burke

"Resistance is not futile, but the most constructive and noble stance of all." Lew Rockwell (lewrockwell.com)

Contents

Part 1:

Introduction

First, CONGRATULATIONS to Mr. Trump for winning the Nov. 8, 2016 Presidential Election! It is generally agreed that he tapped the ignored middle class who were disgusted with the results from the 'Establishment' and the murderous, self-serving, parasites supported by Hillary and her pals! Trumps' promise to 'Drain the Swamp' in DC brought strong support. The Presidents' website is **www.GOP.com**, and all other candidates have their own (use Google search).

I suggest that GOP candidates emphasize the need for major reductions in Federal spending (at home and abroad; emphasize homeland defense, not wars abroad for economic and political goals) to reduce our debt (now over $20 trillion and about 106% of GDP) and avoid a major economic crash (worse than 1932). The US Dollar has been falling in value (purchasing power) since the Federal Reserve System was founded in 1913. The rate of falling has been faster since Nixon went off the gold standard (exchange paper money for real gold) in 1971. It has lost 98% since 1913, of which a 10-times loss or more occurred for most things since 1971. An example is that a family car cost about $2,000 in the 70s and is $20,000 in 2017. We must acknowledge that the USA is a failing Empire (Chapter 2), and is increasing our massive debt with fake money from the Federal Reserve System (Chapter 3 and Table 2). These are the biggest problems, followed by the 33 Issues shown in Chapter 4. **Please read the first 4 Issues right now!;** they are the basic principles I suggest you should follow.

As shown in the Dedication on p. 5, only about 5% (16 million) citizens in America are worried about the trend of our government toward a socialist police-state, where the government at all levels has major control of business, and the lives of the citizens. All of these controls are strongly enforced by the police, and sometimes abusively. Rapid changes in policy are needed to stop these trends before we crash over the economic and cultural cliff!

The purpose of this book is to provide useful info and ideas to help Republican candidates WIN! It applies to all levels (city, county, state, and Federal/Congress), in all 50 states. In particular, for the most powerful office, we want to influence President Trump and his team to adopt some, or all, of the free-market, limited government, sound money, and non-interventionist foreign policy ideas presented in this book. We agree with most of Pres. Trumps policies, and where we disagree with the discussions will be kept private so no damage is done to support for the Trump administration.

The above 5% are a big part of the amazing 'surprise' support that elected Mr. Trump on Nov. 8, 2016! The 5% are worried and angry about the 'Establishment' (Oligarch bosses = Rich and powerful) and its' self-serving welfare-warfare mode of operation. Now we need to convert a big part of the 60% inactive people, and 35% seeking benefits, to our policies. The Republican Party members are mentioned herein because Mr. Trump will need them for much of his success.

Our first major advance was Mr. Trump winning the GOP nomination as the Republican candidate for U.S. President, and his acceptance speech on July 21, 2016! Mr. Trumps' selection of Gov. Mike Pence, of Indiana, as Vice-Presidential candidate on July 16 was well received as a solid addition to the team. He brings a record of supporting conservative issues, including sound money.

Causes of Problems: Before getting into more details about Mr. Trump and his campaign, lets' look at how our countrys' war and welfare policies got us into the damaging messes below. These are the classic traits of a failing Empire! (more in Chapter 2). **The key causes are:**

1) The economic cost of building and maintaining Empire-USA (created by bombing, invading and occupying foreign nations), thus **creating refugees and terrorists** (angry and desperate locals). Our invasions have been for economic and political goals (not defense), and were based on lies by the US President about threats and harm to the US. The same applies to all of our wars since the 1776 Revolution! (see link 'Wars Lies and the Lies..' at App. 1, P.155). In addition to the government buying war goods, and caring for troops, we import excessive and amounts of low cost foreign consumer goods, which leads to exporting jobs and factories, all paid for by new fiat paper or digital money created 'out of thin-air by our central bank, the Federal Reserve System! **The solution is to stop invading other nations, end Empire-USA, and convert to the Gold Standard (coins are the money)**!

2) The cost of social unrest caused by citizen and immigrant demands for more welfare, multiculturalism, etc., and the blow-back of citizens' anger at the police for years of abusive treatment (especially since 2000). Police have become para-military (citizens are the enemy), and resist reforms. Examples of abusive use of laws are; 1) 'Asset Forfeiture', where assets are taken without an arrest or probable cause, and retained or sold by the police, and 2) Excessive use of SWAT (Special Weapons and Tactics), and abuse of the targeted places and people!

3) The decline in value of the U.S. Dollar (USD) caused by creating too many new fake (fiat) US dollars (increasing the money supply), which for now is still the worlds' primary 'reserve currency' (thus any Seller will accept it), to pay for 1 and 2 above. This 'monetary inflation' causes; 1) 'price Inflation' because all existing Dollars become 'worth less' (2 words) in purchasing power, and 2) offshoring of jobs because we import so much from low-wage and low-regulation businesses abroad.

There is almost no limit for the issuer of the worlds' primary reserve currency (anyone will accept and hold it) to create more new fiat money, and it always leads to massive spending and debt for the issuing nation (now our USA, see Table 1 on p. 46 for more). Use of gold will stop this because it cannot be made 'out of thin air' like paper notes. There will always be 'enough' gold because its purchasing power per gram will increase with more demand. See details in Chapter 3.

4) The unconstitutional ObamaCare health plan, started in 2010, has all of the bad traits of high cost, low choice, and no competition one should expect from a socialistic, government-controlled plan. I recommend my free-market plan proposed in Issue #8 in chapter 4, p. 75.

For my part, I have been active in promoting traditional Conservative Principles since my run for Congress in CA District 1 with Pres. Reagan in 1984, and have a letter of support from him (see Appendix 3, P. 164). To help 'spread the word' on the benefits of 'limited government', under a constitution, and with sound money, this book, and my others on government and our monetary system, are This book is available at a leading on-line service. Other books by Dave are there also. The text of this book, and two about money and investing, are posted free at parts 1 and 2 in the left margin of the my site **Forward-USA.org**.

As more people become concerned about the likely crash of the US Dollars' (USD) value (purchasing power), and thus our economy, we will have mass support to bring pressure on Congress to make changes in our national policies. People 'get involved' when they are at risk, so I hope we can implement these traditional principles of;

a) More liberty, free enterprise, and personal responsibility,
b) Limited government with low tax-and-spend policies,
c) Comply with the Constitution, and promote the rule of law (no Imperial Presidency!),
d) Strong defense of our Homeland, but no wars for political and economic goals; i.e., end Empire-USA.
e) A foreign policy of: a) non-intervention abroad (no non-defense wars for Empire-USA), b) end most foreign bases and all foreign aid (usually bribery for control), including money (cash gifts and unpaid loans), and c) end special privileges, (use of our military, extra money, access to our political system, etc.) to any nation, including Israel.
f) Support 'sound money', which means convert the USD to a gold standard as discussed in Chapter 3.

There will be no Fed, no 'U.S. dollar' (USD); the weight of 24 ct gold in a coin (alloys are ok) will be the 'unit of account' for pricing; paper notes are OK for convenience, but must be redeemable by the Issuer in gold to any bearer on demand. This ending of the governments' ability to make new money 'out of thin air' will force reduced spending and debt, and also help solve the problem of excessive imports (we would run out of money) and the offshoring of jobs and factories. Once a major nation converts to gold, all nations will have to since no seller will accept their trash paper! There will always be 'enough' gold because its' value per gram will increase as demand grows against a near-fixed supply (only 2-3% new gold is added annually; by mining, melting jewelry, etc.). See Chapter 5.

*** End of 'Causes' ***

These principles will bring more liberty, peace, prosperity, justice, and morality (more honesty and courtesy; less force, theft and fraud) to the USA and the world.

Sadly, our nation has strayed into 'big government' in the last 84 years since FDR declared in 1933 that all citizens would be cared for by his 'New Deal'! Since 1997, was the 'Project for a New American Century' (now 'newamericancentury.org'), and replaced by 'Foreign Policy Initiative' (FPI.org), written by 'big government conservatives', 'neoconservatives' (see p. 29, led by Cheney and his neo gang, including Steve Forbes and Jeb Bush), and foreign lobbies, has promoted wars for empire abroad (Afghan, Iraq, etc.), and restriction of liberty and rights at home. Their ideas formed the core of the deadly, disastrous, G. Bush foreign policy. They were aided by self-serving, vote-seeking, career politicians who promote welfare and subsidy programs that create dependency and reduce our work-ethic and productivity. The above folks form the 'swamp' that Mr. Trump wants to drain! Too many people see government as 'funder of all nice things', and that it's OK to pay for it with other people's money! That is immoral 'gang-theft-by-vote' funding.

The 'New World Order', 'fiat money', and 'pre-emptive wars' promoted by Nixon and the Bushes led the USA decline into wars for economic (oil) and political (defense of Israel, control of nations) goals **This is an abuse of our troops, so support them by bringing them home!** We pay more than our share for the UN, NATO, and other aging (maybe obsolete or none-of-our-business) political orgs, and we should seek more from our 'partners' or terminate our membership.

The election of Donald Trump should be made into a turning point to end our economic and social decline. Hence my 'Forward USA' plan in Chapter 5.

My plan has no 'privileged groups' (business or human) and brings more Liberty, peace, prosperity, justice and morality (more honesty and courtesy; less force, theft and fraud) to all Americans! 'Fairness' will be defined as allowing people to keep what they have honestly and legally earned through work and initiative.

Remember; 'The government's proper role is to PROTECT the rights of its citizens, as individuals, from violation or threat by OTHERS', not to 'manage' the Economy, the People, and Create Empire-USA!' Sadly, our government has become the biggest boss and abuser in the world.

Trumps' '100 Day Plan'

Pres. Trump, VP Pence, and their staff created a powerful ground-breaking 'contract with voters' called **'A 100 Day Plan to Make America Great Again – For ALL Americans!'** which was presented by Mr. Trump at a meeting in Gettysburg, PA on Oct. 22, 2016.

He said: **On the first day of my term of office,** my administration will immediately pursue the following six measures to clean up the corruption and special interest collusion in Washington, DC:

- **FIRST**, propose a Constitutional Amendment to impose term limits on all members of Congress; (for more, go to p. xx, #27)
- **SECOND**, a hiring freeze on all federal employees to reduce federal workforce through attrition (exempting military, public safety, and public health);
- **THIRD,** a requirement that for every new federal regulation, two existing regulations must be eliminated;
- **FOURTH**, a 5 year-ban on White House and Congressional officials becoming lobbyists after they leave government service;
- **FIFTH**, a lifetime ban on White House officials lobbying on behalf of a foreign government;
- **SIXTH,** a complete ban on foreign lobbyists raising money for American elections.

On the same day, I will begin taking the following seven actions to protect American workers:

- **FIRST,** I will announce my intention to renegotiate NAFTA or withdraw from the deal under Article 2205
- **SECOND,** I will announce our withdrawal from the Trans-Pacific Partnership
- **THIRD,** I will direct my Secretary of the Treasury to label China a currency manipulator
- **FOURTH,** I will direct the Secretary of Commerce and U.S. Trade Representative to identify all foreign trading abuses that unfairly impact American workers and direct them to use every tool under American and international law to end those abuses immediately
- **FIFTH,** I will lift the restrictions on the production of $50 trillion dollars' worth of job-producing American energy reserves, including shale, oil, natural gas and clean coal.
- **SIXTH,** lift the Obama-Clinton roadblocks and allow vital energy infrastructure projects, like the Keystone Pipeline, to move forward
- **SEVENTH,** cancel billions in payments to U.N. climate change programs and use the money to fix America's water and environmental infrastructure

Additionally, on the first day, I will take the following five actions to restore security and the constitutional rule of law:

- **FIRST,** cancel every unconstitutional executive action, memorandum and order issued by Pres. Obama. (Insert; most were not pre-approved by Congress as required)
- **SECOND,** begin the process of selecting a replacement for Justice Scalia from one of the 20 judges on my list, who will uphold and defend the Constitution of the United States (Insert; Not biased as 'conservative' or 'Liberal')
- **THIRD,** cancel all federal funding to Sanctuary Cities
- **FOURTH,** begin removing the more than 2 million criminal illegal immigrants from the country and cancel visas to foreign countries that won't take them back
- **FIFTH,** suspend immigration from terror-prone regions where vetting cannot safely occur. All vetting of people coming into our country will be considered extreme vetting.

Next, Pres. Trump said: I will work with Congress to introduce the following broader legislative measures and fight for their passage within the first 100 days.

1. **Middle Class Tax Relief And Simplification Act**.:An economic plan designed to grow the economy 4% per year and create at least 25 million new jobs through massive tax reduction and simplification, in combination with trade reform, regulatory relief, and lifting the restrictions on American energy. The largest tax reductions are for the middle class. A middle-class family with 2 children will get a 35% tax cut. The current number of brackets will be reduced from 7 to 3, and tax forms will likewise be greatly simplified. The business rate will be lowered from 35 to 15 percent, and the trillions of dollars of American corporate money overseas can now be brought back at a 10 percent rate.

2. **End The Offshoring Act.:** Establishes tariffs to discourage companies from laying off their workers in order to relocate in other countries and ship their products back to the U.S. tax-free. (for more, go to part 2 in L margin of Forward-USA.org. Convert to gold as money to end excessive imports and resultant offshoring. No tariffs.)

3. **American Energy & Infrastructure Act.** : Leverages public-private partnerships, and private investments through tax incentives, to spur $1 trillion in infrastructure investment over 10 years. It is revenue neutral.

4. **School Choice and Education Opportunity Act.** : Redirects education dollars to gives parents the right to send their kid to the public, private, charter, magnet, religious, or home school of their choice. Ends Common Core, and brings supervision to local communities. It expands vocational and technical education, and make 2 and 4-year colleges more

affordable.

5. **Repeal and Replace Obamacare Act** : My plan; 1) fully repeals Obamacare and replaces it with Health Savings Accounts, 2) includes the ability to purchase health insurance across state lines, and 3) lets states manage Medicaid funds.

Reforms will also include cutting the red tape at the FDA: there are over 4,000 drugs awaiting approval, and we especially want to speed the approval of life-saving medications. (Insert by Redick; Should also end the licensing and pricing monopoly of State Boards so pricing will become competitive, and b) give nurses more authority to work alone as 'Physicians Assistants'.   (Read item 8 'Health Care' in Chapter 4.)

6. **Affordable Childcare and Eldercare Act**. Allows Americans to deduct childcare and elder care from their taxes, incentivizes employers to provide on-site childcare services, and creates tax-free Dependent Care Savings Accounts for both young and elderly dependents, with matching contributions for low-income families.

7. **End Illegal Immigration Act** Fully-funds the construction of a wall on our southern border with the full understanding that Mexico will be reimbursing the United States for the full cost of such wall; establishes a 2-year mandatory minimum federal prison sentence for illegally re-entering the U.S. after a previous deportation, and a 5-year mandatory minimum for illegally re-entering for those with felony convictions, multiple misdemeanor convictions or two or more prior deportations; also reforms visa rules to enhance penalties for overstaying and to ensure open jobs are offered to American workers first. (Go to p. 99 and read #17)

8. **Restoring Community Safety Act**. Reduces surging crime, drugs and violence by creating a Task Force on Violent Crime and increasing funding for programs that train and assist local police; increases resources for federal law enforcement agencies and federal prosecutors to dismantle criminal gangs and put violent offenders behind bars.

9. **Restoring National Security Act**. Rebuilds our military by eliminating the defense sequester and expanding military investment. Provides Veterans with the ability to receive public VA treatment or attend the private doctor of their choice; protects our vital infrastructure from cyber-attack; establishes new screening procedures for immigration to ensure those who are admitted to our country support our people and our values

10. '**Clean up Corruption in Washington' Act**. Enacts new ethics reforms to Drain the Swamp and reduce the corrupting influence of special interests on our politics.

He continued: "On November 8th, Americans will be voting for this 100-day plan to restore prosperity to our economy, security to our communities, and honesty to our government. This is my pledge to you. If we follow these steps, we will once more have a government of, by and for the people."

The 100-Day plan is great, but **lacks a plan for; 1) conversion of the US Dollar to gold, 2) termination of the 'Federal Reserve System', and 3) end invasion of nations that not threatened or harmed us (i.e, end Empire building).** The Forward USA team has created a plan using a commodity (such as gold) as money (by weight), which limits the governments'

---

ability to recklessly expand the money supply to fund wars, welfare, excessive imports, and corruption. No wonder politicians don't like gold! Read the 5-step plan for conversion of the Dollar to gold coins (valued by weight of 24 ct gold) in the '**Monetary Revolution USA'** book at Part 2 in the left margin of www.Forward-USA.org. A related book, 'How to Protect and Grow Your Wealth', is there also and includes investment ideas. Both are in the 'books' section of Amazon.com under my name. I will appreciate you feedback.

Trumps Cabinet and Team Appointments

Mr. Trumps' first appointments, starting in June-2015 when he announced his candidacy, were his Campaign Manager and staff, followed on July 16, 2016 by the excellent choice of Mike Pence, Gov. of IN and former U.S. Congressman, as his VP running mate. Trump won the Presidential nomination at the Republican Party convention in Cleveland, OH on July 19, 2016. He then commenced to recruit his personal staff. The first two major announcements were appointment on **November 13, 2016** of Steve Bannon as Trumps' 'Chief Strategist and Senior Counselor' and Reince Priebus as 'White House Chief of Staff.' The choice of Priebus, a loyal campaign ally to Trump who has close ties with House of Representatives Speaker Paul Ryan, signalled Trumps' willingness to work with Ryan and the Republican-led Congress to get his agenda passed. Bannon is controversial because of; 1) his work as 'Executive Chairman' of Breitbart News LLC., which is perceived as an 'alt-right' news source, plus 2) his 'in your face' attitude toward self-serving career politicians. Bannons' position takes about half of the 'White House Chief of Staffs' former work and authority. Names of Cabinet Secretaries have been discussed, but require Congressional approval. See the complete list of staff and Cabinet names, with brief bios, in Appendix 4 on p. 165.

(Reserved)

Chapter 1
USA Status: Economics and Politics

This chapter presents a comprehensive analysis of the status and trends in the USA economy and Federal government. It discusses the cause-and-effect correlation between: 1. Government violation of our rights and the Constitution, and international law (aggressive invasions of nations, not defense) and 2. The corruption (illegal acts) and abuses (improper use of authority), and economic collapse we see around us in the USA, and worldwide.

Complacent citizens deserve the government abuse they tolerate, good and hard! The opposite of complacency is responsible activism. If you like the ideas in this book, DO SOMETHING!, such as become a candidate for local or national office, write letters of complaint and suggestion to government officials, donate to a favorite candidate or Republican group, etc. This book pulls no punches, and goes to the heart of our social and economic problems, and how to solve them.

On the economic front, excessive spending and debt by both the people and government have placed our nation on the brink of collapse. Under 'normal' financial conditions, the people and government would run out of money and stop spending, but as discussed below and in Chapter 3, the US Dollar is the world's primary reserve currency (all Sellers and Lenders will accept and hold them) so we alone can create paper and digital dollars out of thin air to pay our bills. The Bush-Obama-Bernanke style bailout and stimulus plans only prolong the pain by engaging in more spending and debt to save a corrupt and unsustainable system (often led by their friends and campaign donors) that should instead be reformed and replaced. The greedy and abusive Wall Street and business managers are saved and the good managers end up with taxpayer-financed competitors who should be gone!

Goldman Sachs (or Golden Sacks) had two of their top people (Rubin and Paulson) in DC as Treasurer for Clinton and Bush, and guess what, they got lots of bailout money directly plus about $30 bill. of the bailout money given to AIG. Talk about favors to friends! Sounds like fraud and theft to me. The people are largely ignored in this process, and end up paying the bills by taxes and less-valuable money (less purchasing power), while the value of their savings shrink and jobs disappear. Now former Golden Sacks officer Gary Cohn is Director of the Presidents' Economic Council (P. 176).

We recommend that the government stay out of the recovery process and let the free market penalize and eliminate the self-serving, counter-productive, managers with loss of their jobs and trimming or bankruptcy of their firms. Those who used illegal methods should be arrested! Iceland set the example by letting the banks fail, and prosecuting the corrupt managers! (no other nation did!) This is painful, but allows recovery to start sooner and better.

'Free Market' is briefly defined as: 'Little or no government control of pricing, creation of new firms, pay and benefits, hiring and firing, etc.' (see p. 178), all within the Core Principle in Chapter 4, # 2, and the Constitution. This is the approach preferred by the **'Austrian School' of economic thought** (Hayek, von Mises, Rothbard; Glossary P. 177), which emphasizes the spontaneous organizing power of free market pricing, decisions by individuals, gold-as-money, and little or no government management or stimulation of the economy. Liberals prefer the **'Keynesian Theory'** (Krugman, Samuelson, Stiglitz, Bernanke; P. 177) which depends on massive use of government fiscal (spending) and monetary (interest rates, money supply) policy, both using fake money, to try to create prosperity or avoid and end depressions by 'stimulus' spending. History and logic show the Keynes approach is unsustainable and never works for more than a year or two. Monetary stimulus is like heroin; it gives you a brief high, but has no long-term benefit and then makes you sick (a 'bubble burst' recession, etc.!)

For another definition, I define '**Greed**' (P. 168) as an excessive desire for advantage or benefits that ends up hurting the seeker. Examples are: 1. investing in high-risk securities and losing, or 2. working so hard that you hurt your health and family. This is not to be confused with **'Success'**, where the seeker gains in a productive, lawful, sustainable, and ethical way. Liberals and Progressives often view them as the same. See full definitions in the Glossary, P. 166.

Pres. Obama's national health care system ('The Patient Protection and Affordable Care Act' -PPACA-, or 'ObamaCare') was announced in early 2010, and took effect during 2014. It is costing far more than predicted, thus adding a huge debt and tax burden, while reducing the quality of health care (rationing of services, delays, impersonal). I know because I have lived in Canada under their 'single payer' government system (no competition between providers, less equipment, poor courtesy). Read more in Chapter 4, item 8. As shown in Chapters 4 and 5, we must revise and repeal many laws in order to **Rebuild America.** For updates, go to Daves' web site **www.Forward-USA.org**.

As described more in Chapter 3 'Fake Money', our unique position as **issuer of the primary world reserve currency** (anyone will accept and keep it; good as gold). **That means we can create new money to pay our bills! No other nation can do this,** and it has allowed us to create hundreds of billions of US Dollars (USD) out of thin air (now we do it by trillions!) to finance subprime mortgages and pay for imports (leading to 'off-shoring' jobs), wars, pork, bailouts, stimulus, etc. The corruption and abuses could not be done without this flood of fake money. It is the evil root that funds most corruption and abuse. But politicians and bankers love it, so it keeps flowing! This excessive expansion of the money supply ('monetary inflation', like a balloon) reduces the value of all other USD, and risks eventual collapse of its value (when people, firms and nations finally refuse to accept or keep it). A group called the BRICS (Brazil, Russia, India, China, and S. Africa) has been using their own currencies between each other for several years. As this grows, demand for the USD will fall, and it will lose value!

The purchasing power (PP) of the USD has dropped by 98% since the Federal Reserve System was created in 1913. The drop has been sharpest since Nixon took us off the last remnants of the gold standard in 1971 (we were running out due to redemptions by other nations). The gold standard requires that paper notes are redeemable for gold; and prices are by weight (grams) of 24 ct gold (not 'dollars'-USD), which limits excessive creation of USD. Government and private spending has zoomed up since 1971 as new money flooded our economy. Prices go up as the Dollar's value (PP) goes down, and wages seldom keep up with the higher prices. On a personal level, this is why we see more wives working to help meet family expenses.

The nations that accumulate USDs from payments for exports to us, often use them to buy our government debt ('Treasuries'; T-Bills, bonds, etc.) as a way to earn some interest. China and Japan alone hold 23 % of America's over $18 trillion federal debt. As of Feb-2015, China had about $2.2 trillion invested in dollar assets (the world's biggest holder), of which about $1.3 tn are in US Treasuries. This is about 70% of China's total reserves (down from 80% in 2002), and they are starting to use them to buy resource assets (mines, oil/gas rights) worldwide to avoid losses as value of the USD drops. Maybe they will buy the U.S. Congress next? Like all politicians, most are 'for sale', as discussed below.

The abuse by the USA of its monetary system is a major world concern, and has been the main topic of the annual G20 meetings since April-2009 (more on P. 1). Other nations are looking for ways to avoid dependency on, and ownership of, USDs. A flight to safety is starting, and could lead to a collapse in USD value (fake money requires demand to support its' PP). Russia and China have suggested the USD be replaced as the reserve currency by a 'basket' of several currencies, or Special Drawing Rights managed by the International Monetary Fund (IMF). Details are shown here: http://www.activistpost.com/2016/10/elite-leaders-want-new-reserve-currency-crash-dollar.html .

The BRICS (Brazil, Russia, India, China, and South Africa) started trading with each other in their own currencies in 2011, thus reducing demand for the USD, and speeding its fall in value! If we keep spending and borrowing (increasing our deficits and debt) too much, and keep creating new money (inflate the money supply) to pay for it; 1. The USD will crash in purchasing power (PP), 2. We will not be able to afford foreign purchases with our soon near-worthless paper money, 3. Interest rates will soar for our debt, and 4. We will pay existing foreign debts and interest with the same near-worthless paper money. This is debt default by hyperinflation. No country wants this to happen, especially our creditors and holders of cash and USD denominated assets. Thus they discuss alternatives for a smooth departure from the current dependency on the USD as the primary reserve currency for world trade.

As discussed in Chapter 2, Empire-USA is an expensive and damaging part of our foreign policy. On May 8, 2009, Ivan Eland Ph.D. (Independent.org) wrote in his article, 'How the US Empire Contributed to the Economic Crisis', "A few — and only a few — prescient commentators have questioned whether the U.S. can sustain its informal global empire in the wake of the most severe economic crisis since World War II. And the simultaneous quagmires in Iraq and Afghanistan are leading more and more opinion leaders and taxpayers to this question. But the U.S. Empire helped cause the meltdown in the first place.

War has a history of causing financial and economic calamities. It does so directly by almost always causing price inflation — that is, too much money chasing too few goods. During wartime, governments usually commandeer resources from the private sector into the government realm to fund the fighting. This action leaves shortages of resources to make consumer goods and their components, therefore pushing prices up. Making things worse, governments often times print money to fund the war, thus adding to the amount of money chasing the smaller number of consumer goods. Such 'make-believe' wealth has funded many U.S. wars." These observations also tie in with Chapter 3; 'Fake Money ...'.

In the political arena, we find most Congresspersons, party leaders, and 'loyalist' workers (at the DC, State and County levels) of the major political parties have failed the people, and should be replaced! This group is called the 'Establishment'! The priority of most of them is to keep their Party jobs and social and business connections! They want to be viewed as 'normal' and 'loyal', so they are obedient, follow-the-leader, party-first, and denounce critics of their Party and its leaders as wierdos, conspiracy theorists, and disloyal troublemakers. I observe that over 90% of US citizens who vote pick the person they think will help get them what they want from government (cash, benefits, legal favors, etc.). The same applies to campaign donors who expect a payback if their candidate is elected (they often donate to both opposing candidates). The Main-Stream-Media (MSM) follows the same cowardly path (to avoid offense to subscribers and advertisers).

Those nation-first, people-first, 'comply with the Constitution' rebels (like me) who dare to question the Establishment Party Lines are shunned and ridiculed. Thus the misconduct of those in power gets worse, and the Party declines in membership and at the polls. The Republican Party and mainstream media (MSM) treatment of 2008 and 2012 Presidential candidate Rep. Ron Paul (R-TX) is a good example. Despite his popular support and strong fundraising, he was excluded from most TV debates and the national and several state conventions because he dared to question our interventionist foreign policy (for oil and Empire-USA), excessive spending at home and abroad, and unconstitutional laws. During the Aug-2012 GOP convention in Tampa, Dr. Paul and his supporters were cheated and abused via intimidation, and fraudulent rule changes to prevent seating of his delegates!

There was great concern that Mr. Trump would get the same treatment in Cleveland, but fortunately Mr. Priebus followed to rules and Mr. Trump was declared the primary winner, despite a last minute effort by the #NeverTrump group. This is part of the reason Priebus was appointed Trump's Chief of Staff on Nov. 13, 2016!

'Establishment' leaders such as G. W. Bush, M. Romney, McCain, and Kasich did not attend, hoping they could take-over after a blowup against Trump! It didn't work!

Most party leaders toe-the-line to avoid disturbing the party's 'image', and upsetting major campaign donors, most of whom profit or grow from war, subsidies, and special laws and rulings ('crony capitalism'). As an activist for better (usually less) government since 1978 (I ran for Congress with Reagan in 1984 and have a support letter from him, P. 151), I have watched with dismay as my party has been taken-over since 1988 by far-right 'neo-conservatives' and the religious right. This created the 'Big Government Conservative' concept (with its spending and 'pre-emptive' Mideast wars; Afghan, Iraq, Libya; Iran soon?) for oil, empire, and defense of Israel, all of which violate the Constitution and Republican principles. The Heritage Foundation leads this thinking, including Trustee Steve Forbes, and their awards to warmonger Dick Cheney.

Our 'exceptional' role as the world's policeman (or 'Boss'), and ruler of 'Empire USA' are huge issues that need to be discussed. Just as with Rome, and all other empires in history (see Chapter 2), the expense of wars abroad and welfare at home caused their failure. The USA is on the brink, and we need the plan "Rebuild America' shown in Chapter 5.

My plan promotes traditional Republican values and principles as represented by Taft, Goldwater, Kemp, and Reagan. We oppose the government handing-out favors to anyone, liberal or conservative, business or personal.
They are all un-constitutional and depend on funding from gang-theft-by-vote, or fake money from the Fed (a hidden tax), and usually do more harm than good (counting side effects). **Private (voluntary) charity and free enterprise (with laws against fraud and theft), work best**.
This approach is moral and sustainable! We follow the Core Principle shown in Chapter 4, Item 2 which says the government should only 'protect rights', which means 'natural rights', not 'legislated rights'.

Most elected officials, especially in Congress with its unlimited supply of fake money, will do almost anything to keep their plush and powerful jobs. The pork, earmark grants, subprime loans, and favors to campaign donors are part of their career planning. Rome called it 'bread and circuses'. Their failure to end the tragic and illegal 'non-defense' Iraq and Afghan wars during the 2006 to 2008 Democratic 'mandate' years is a shameful example. The Dems would rather have thousands more people die (our troops and many times more local civilians) than be blamed for a messy withdrawal after our illegal, immoral invasion and occupation. Shame on them!!

Excessive spending and debt loomed as threats to the U.S. economy, and Congress and Bush ignored the problems! These chickens came home to roost in 2008 and 2012 with the election of Obama. More and more State projects are funded (pork, grants) and controlled by the federal government because it never runs out of fake money. The state politicians beg for it and states' rights get weaker due to the strings attached. The U.S. debt (Treasury Bills and Bonds) is over $18 trillion and grew by leaps with the QE-1, 2, 3 bailout and stimulus programs! Worse, this does not count the 'off-budget', unfunded, over $15 tn dollar future liabilities of Social Security, $99 tn for Medicare, and $9 tn for Obamacare (P. 36 and more at **www.pgpf.org** and USDebtClock.org). These debts can only be paid by massive creation of more dollars, which will reduce the value of all dollars, and cause an inflationary depression!! We are 'stuck between a rock and a hard place', and only a major reduction in spending and benefits will solve the problem. For more info on money, go to Chapters 3 and 5

Neocon warmongers drove our foreign policy in the Bush-43 years. The 'Project for a New American Century' (PNAC, **www.newamericancentury.org**) was founded by 'use more power' pushers such as neocons (new conservatives) Cheney, Rumsfeld, Perle, Kristol, Abrams, Feith, and the like (to their shame, even Jeb Bush and Steve Forbes were members!). Their plan, produced in September of 1997, was "Rebuilding

America's Defenses: Strategy, Forces and Resources for a New Century". It depends on war to defend and expand Empire-USA control world-wide, and became the blueprint for the Bush team to invade Iraq and Afghanistan (for oil, Israel, and bases). The 9/11 tragedy was the trigger they needed! (see items 4 and 5 in Chapter 4). In Mar-2009 they changed their name to 'The Foreign Policy Initiative' (**www.foreignpolicyi.org**) with the same plans to grow Empire-USA. Watch them get funding from the military-industrial folks! Senators such as John McCain, Lindsey Graham and Joe Lieberman fit into the warmonger category with their steady support of wars abroad, and ridicule of those who support a non-interventionist foreign policy. There are others. The firm 'Blackwater Protection', (https://blackwaterprotection.com), led by Erik Prince, is a private security firm that was well paid to do military 'mercenary' work (including killing). This is under legal review.

Many neocons are Israel-First Zionists (and all are Empire builders), which means they put the success of Israel before the USA, and expect the USA to pay for its defense with our blood and treasure. The Israeli lobby AIPAC (American-Israel Public Affairs Committee, **www.aipac.org**) should be registered as a foreign lobby (they claim it is a USA org!), and thus disclose its finances, as those of UK and France are; another special exception for Israel. If a Congressperson doesn't support Israel, they don't get re-elected!! AIPAC attacks them, or supports their opponent. Take note that most Congresspersons (plus Cheney, Rice, Powell, Obama, Romney, etc.) attend their annual banquet in DC and kiss-up by promising vast military and financial support for Israel!! Obama's former Chief of Staff, Rahm Emanuel (now mayor of Chicago), is a dual US-Israeli citizen and served in their army, as did his father. Our dual citizen laws do not allow the citizen to serve in the other country's military, except for Israel! (another privilege). Only a retiring Congressperson will criticize AIPAC. Its intervention in USA affairs is a massive scandal!! No cries of anti-Semitism please; this is a legal, political and financial issue, not religious. For more go to: http://original.antiwar.com/giraldi/2009/05/18/picking-on-aipac/

G. W. Bush and his team 'used' 9/11 and their 'War on Terror' to justify a long list of excess powers for the Executive branch, plus a host of violations of domestic laws and liberties (domestic spying, excess control of travel –TSA, torture and jailing of 'non-combatants', etc.).

John W. Whitehead (www.rutherford.org) wrote an article on Nov. 2, 2012, 'Looking Beyond Election Day (**http://lewrockwell.com/whitehead/whitehead62.1.html**) that shows how our Federal and local governments are abusing our rights. The 'servant' has become 'boss'!

My Plan to Restore American and Republican Principles:

The Republican Party has veered off-course since Nixon abrogated the Bretton Woods Monetary Treaty in 1971 (and imposed price controls), and needs new leadership and reform at all levels. They now condone or promote 'more-government' for war, spending, religion, illegal immigration, unconstitutional restriction of rights, illegal 'signing statements' that change laws, and illegal Executive Orders that start wars, torture, assassination by drone, and corruption! Some say suspensions of rights are 'needed for a while'; Nonsense, the free market and rule of law work best, and the rights rarely come back once ignored!
The religious right, power and resource-seeking (oil) builders of Empire-USA, and 'Israel-first' warmonger neocons now dominate the Republican Party, and push for imposing their views on all of us. True Republicans oppose using the government as a tool to impose ones beliefs on others, and funding your projects with 'gang-theft-by-vote' taxation. We will work to restore the government to only protecting our rights, and not managing or controlling our lives, the economy, and the world! We recommend:
The Plan

1) Limited, Constitution-based government, emphasizing sound money, personal responsibility, Liberty, property rights, low taxing and spending, and a non-interventionist foreign policy, with strong defense against homeland attack and valid threats,
2) No wars (or 'Police actions') without the express approval of Congress,
3) No pre-emptive wars or invasions,
4) Use war only for defense of homeland from invasions or proven threats. No foreign wars or invasions for economic or political goals (such as for oil, land, defense of Israel, and Empire-USA; see Appendix 1, P. 131), and
5) Repeal unconstitutional and unnecessary restrictions on liberty and privacy, and Executive Branch power-grabs, such as the Patriot Act, and the Military Commissions Act, and restore Habeas Corpus.
It is time to repudiate the misconduct, and violation of Republican Principles by our 'leaders' (past and present), and start an honest rebuilding plan. Rather than continuing the present leadership's mode of avoidance and denial. Donald Trump can lead the way!

Fighting the system is hard, but I predict Ghandhi's aphorism will prevail: **"First they ignore you, then they ridicule you, then they fight you, then you win."**

(Reserved)

Chapter 2: Empire-USA: The Phases and Failures

The USA is the biggest empire in history, and is far into 'Phase 3 – Failure'. Thus, candidates, staff, and elected officials should understand how empires start, grow and fail (they ALL fail!).The analysis shown below explains why all empires, and 'Imperial Style' governments, in history have failed, and why our 'Empire-USA' faces the same fate. The only question is whether the people and government of the USA have the wisdom and will to engage in a 'Managed Decline' by terminating the empire and imperial conduct on their own schedule, rather than by chaotic crash of the US Dollar, economy, and lifestyle. Take notice of the 'Solutions' section in Part C below.

****

The Phases of an Empire

Part A: Key Points

* **An Empire is a nation that; 1. Owns colonies, and/or 2. Controls, or has great influence over, other nations**. Empires require economic and military strength to start and maintain, and this is expensive.

* **All Empires fail, and for the same reasons:** 1. Expense of military abroad, and subsidies at home, 2. Decline in domestic productivity (spoiled, parasitic citizens), and 3. Corruption (illegal conduct) and decadence and abuse (immoral conduct; fraud, theft, etc.) by leaders and citizens.

* Empire-USA, Our Deal to other nations is: 'We will be the world's policeman and protect you, but you must accept our fake money and 'influence'. With our spending for over 800 bases in 130 countries, the USA is far into Phase 3-Failure. Look around you for the symptoms shown in Part B-3 and Part C below.

Part B: Events/Symptoms in each Phase

Phase 1- Growth (shown on chart on page 27)

* Land: Gain territory by 'discovery' (too bad for the natives), or conquest.

* Strength: Start growth of economic and military strength. Sound money (precious metal, or redeemable paper).

* Government: New land is governed as a colony or part of homeland nation (becoming a sovereign republic may require a revolution).

* Ethics: Most government people and citizens are hard-working and honest. Government is a 'servant'.

Phase 2- Maturation

* Land: Add contiguous land, or remote colonies, by conquest, annexation (Hawaii), or negotiation.

* Strength: Become a world leader in both economic and military strength. Homeland receives cheap imports from colonies. Currency is debased to allow more government spending, without raising taxes.

* Government: Grows stronger and acts as boss, manager, nanny, owner, etc. Power is used to 'manage' other nations to impose/protect the Empire's 'interests'.

* Ethics: Corruption and decadence grow due to decline in personal responsibility caused by nanny state.

Figure 1: The Phases of an Empire
Chart Height Shows Combined Military and Economic Strength (Power and Wealth)

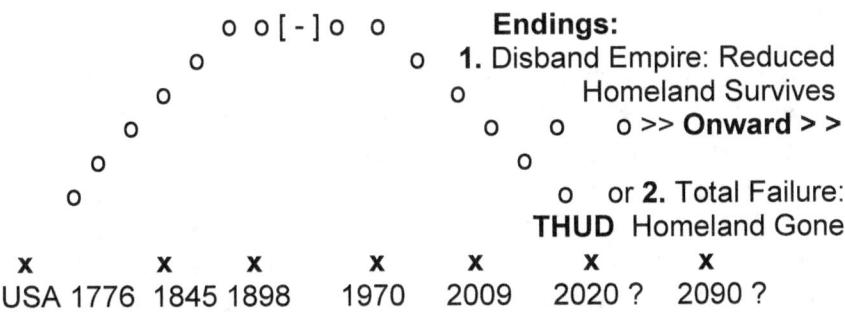

Phase 1, Growth - Phase 2, Mature - Phase 3, Decline or Fail

Phase 3- Decline and/or Failure

* Land: Lose colonies (or control of other nations) by revolution or voluntary release (due to expense and unrest).

* Strength: No longer a world leader. Power declines by 50% or more. Value of fake currency crashes in purchasing power by 50% or more. Default on debt (or pay-off with low value paper currency).

* Government: Gets weak and desperate. Leaders try to gain power to survive citizen discontent. 'Bread and Circuses' grow, now called grants, subsidies, stimulus, and entitlements.

* Ethics: Corruption and decadence are rampant in both social and government conduct. Failure occurs as either; A. Nation survives, but at a reduced level of strength and standard of living (England, France, Italy, Spain, and Russia are examples; see list in Part D), or B. Ceases to exist due to takeover by other nations or groups.

Part C: Empire-USA is in Phase 3: Decline or Failure

Problems:

* **High Expenses**: The expense to maintain bases, and fight wars, worldwide exceeds the monetary and political benefits. As of late 2014, the US has over 800 military bases, with troops (not counting embassies), in 130 countries, and acts as the world's policeman (Boss?) to protect its 'interests', and impose 'influence'. Resistance by our 'subjects' is building. Military expenses are a drag on the economy, and the troops get less than ideal equipment due to cost problems. Host nations are unhappy having our occupying troops.

* **High Debt:** The US is a bankrupt Empire by any measure. It cannot hope to pay back the about $9 trillion in debt held by other nations, or the about $141 trillion unfunded future obligations of domestic programs (Medicare, Social Security, pensions, etc.; see p. 36). Interest payments are huge. As of early 2017 the US Dollar (USD) is still the world's primary 'reserve currency' (used and held as 'good as gold' by other nations; it can be viewed as a share in 'USA Inc.'), but declining in its percent use worldwide (was 80%, now 60%) because the US is also the world's biggest debtor, and has high deficits. **This combination of 'fiat' paper currency (not made of, or convertible to, gold or silver) with reserve status has never occurred before in history!** Thus, since all US government debt is denominated in USD, the government can create new low-value dollars out of thin air to pay its debts! A new form of default! The USD is in a precarious position due to excessive expansion of the money supply ('inflation') and the USD could crash in value at any time. The extreme is 'hyperinflation', when the money becomes almost worthless. As with heroin, lots of fake money (the Federal Reserve Bank calls it 'liquidity' or 'quantitative easing') feels good at first, but has withdrawal pain called recession or depression. Since the federal government never runs out of money, it often becomes the funder for state projects (with strings attached, called 'control'), and states' rights wither. This gives vote-getting power to Congressmen, and acquiescent State officials suck it up to avoid taxing to raise state funds.

* **Enemies:** The US claims to be a 'world leader', but this is often a cover to be a bully to control other countries with an occupying force to gain land and resources (mostly oil). This started in 1812 with the failed invasion of Canada, then 1845 with the Mexican-American War, and 1898 with the Spanish-American war (which led to occupation/acquisition of the Philippines) and 'annexation' of Hawaii. The World Wars, Korea, Vietnam and others followed.

The Balkans, Afghan, Iraq, and Libyan wars are primarily about; 1. Control of oil (The US wants it all; no 'easy-cheap' Mid East oil for Russia, India and China), 2. Defense of Israel, 3. Land for bases to control the greater mideast, and 4. Continuation of oil sales in US Dollars by Iraq and Iran. The Ukraine activity is to suppress the growing power Russia. The US entered (started) all these wars based on lies by U.S. leaders. What a disgrace and ripoff of the people and their foreign victims! Trust and respect for the US has declined in the eyes of its citizens and other nations. This meddling foreign policy contributed to 9/11 and terror. The federal government grasps for new, unconstitutional power.

* **Corruption and Bad Ethics:** Ethics and social conduct are on the decline in the US. Corruption is rampant in both the government and business. Shady conduct is considered 'normal' (gang theft by vote, 'earmark' pork handouts, lying, etc.). Prime time TV and movies are now riddled with sexual content, cursing, glorification of misconduct ('The Sopranos', 'Desperate Housewives', etc.), and violence (NASCAR, cop shows). Sports are riddled with violence (the fans like it!) and cheating, condoned by coaches and team owners that want to sell more tickets. Little or none of the above occurred in the '50s. It is typical conduct in a failing empire, as social mores decline.

Solutions: Of the two ways to end the inevitable Phase 3 of an Empire (Decline or Failure), it is far less painful to engage in a 'managed decline', or 'nation restoration', compared to a massive depression. England and France are examples.

A 'managed' process is shown in Chapter 5, which includes prompt action to;

1. Invoke a major **change in foreign policy** by; a. Terminating Empire-USA, and its role as policeman and bully of the world, and focus on homeland defense; b Reducing spending and conflict by closing most, or all, overseas bases, and keeping only a minimal standing army (primarily State-controlled National Guard); c. Stop creating enemies by meddling in the affairs of other nations by force, sanctions, or bribery (no preemptive wars or occupations); and d. Promote free trade.

2. Invoke a similar **change in domestic policy** where; a. Federal spending is reduced by 50% or more; b. Creation of new fake money is ended; c. Sound money is introduced (paper is convertible to precious metal), and the Federal Reserve System is abolished; d. The Constitution and law are adhered to (with repeal of recent bad laws); and e. Market intervention (favors to firms, unions, people) is ended, and free enterprise capitalism is used.

These steps would help bring the government back to its proper role to; **'Protect the personal and property rights of citizens, as individuals, from threat or violation by others'**. With this approach, the USA and its citizens would enjoy a future of peace, prosperity, justice and good ethics. It always works! I cite W. Germany in 1948, and later Ireland, Prov. of Alberta, Canada, and New Zealand.

Part D: The History of Empire Phases

Sources: 1. 'An Inquiry into the Decline and Fall of Nations', W. Playfair, England, 1805 (Rare books library, Toronto, Canada), 2. 'Empire of Debt', Bonner and Wiggins, 2006

Name	Start Phase 1	End Phase 3	Total Years	Status
Babylonian	1900 bc	1600 bc	300	gone
Assyrian	900 bc	612 bc	288	gone
Carthage	800 bc	100 bc	700	gone
Persian	648 bc	330 bc	318	gone, Iran survived
Athenian-Greek	500 bc	300 bc	200	gone
Macedonian	338 bc	309 bc	29	gone
Chinese	221 bc	1912	233	Homeland survived
Roman	573 bc	476	1,049	gone, split to Byzantine & Holy Roman
Byzantine	1054	1453	399	gone
Arabian	630	1258	628	gone
Holy Roman	800	1806	1006	gone
Portuguese	1495	1975	480	Homeland survived
Mongol	1206	1920	714	gone, Mongolia survived
Abyssinian	1270	1974	704	gone
Ottoman	1281	1923	642	gone, Turkey survived
Spanish	1492	1975	483	Homeland survived
British	1500	1950	450	Homeland survived
French	1600	1965	365	Homeland survived
Netherlands	1627	1944	317	Homeland survived
Austro-Hung.	1804	1918	114	Aust. & Hung. survived
USA	1845	(active)	167 +	In Ph. 3; #1 power
German	1884	1918	34	Homeland survived
Japanese	1871	1945	76	Homeland survived

Chapter 3: Fake Money, How it Funds Wars and Corruption

This chapter is a summary of our monetary system, and its' problems. The complete 'Fake Money' story, including a plan to convert to new gold money, is described at length in my book 'Monetary Revolution-USA'. See the text at part 2 in the left margin of our site Forward-USA.org, or buy it at Amazon.com. See other articles in Appendix 2. Note that I use the terms 'money' and 'currency' as synonymous, but some writers consider 'money' as 'real' (made of gold, or redeemable for gold) and 'currency' as fiat or fake.

After years of successful free-market money (most of 1792 to 1913), the unconstitutional Federal Reserve System (a privately-owned bank; they used 'Federal' to make it sound like a federal agency, and 'System' since many citizens and politicians oppose central banks) was created 'by and for' politicians and bankers in 1913. This gave the federal government a monopoly (via legal tender laws) on creation and 'management' of both metallic and paper money, with the announced purpose of protecting its value. Since then, the US Dollar (USD) has lost 98% of its value (purchasing power)!!
In 1933 President F. D. Roosevelt (FDR) was worried that, a. People would avoid use of his low-value paper money, and b. Foreign countries were concerned about our lack of gold reserves and might start redeeming paper dollars for gold, so by an illegal Executive Order #6102 in April, 1933 he forced all citizens to submit their gold coins and bullion to the government for $20.67 per ounce in paper dollars. Then he decreased the amount of gold backing each paper dollar by illegally re-setting the price of gold to $35 oz. A ripoff! They used part of this profit to fund the Exchange Stabilization Fund (ESF) with $2 bill., which was part of the Gold Reserve Act of 1934. The ESF allows the US Treasurer to 'play the gold market' to keep the price down, so the USD looks better! They used it in 2011 and 2012 to drive gold down from $1,900 to $1,500 oz.

In 1944 the winners of WW2 met at a resort hotel in the Bretton Woods area of Vermont and agreed that only nations could exchange paper money for gold (the 'Bretton Woods Agreement'). In 1965 LBJ ended use of silver in coins and used cheaper copper and nickel alloys. The pre-1965 coins ('junk silver') now sell for their bullion value.

Then Nixon abrogated the Bretton Woods Agreement in August, 1971 because; a) France and other countries were converting their 'EuroDollars' to gold (USD in Europe due to our payment for imports from there), and we were running out; and b) The US was poor after spending on Vietnam and LBJ's 'Great Society', etc.
 Under this pressure, Nixon illegally 'floated' the USD (no fixed-price for gold; no fixed exchange rates with foreign currency), and ended convertibility to gold by any person or government. This meant the U.S. could make dollars out of thin air at will, and did we ever! With the USD no longer 'good as gold', the USD reserves of all other nations lost their gold 'backing', so their currency became fiat by default.

Table 1
Growth of M0: Basic Money Supply   (Billion USD)

Year (Dec.)	M0	Dollar Change	Percent Change	Notes
1918	4.874	0	0	
1920	6.043	1.169	24.0	3
1930	5.949	-0.194	-1.6	4
1940	14.808	8.859	148.9	5
1950	33.033	18.225	123.1	
1960	39.423	6.390	19.3	
1970	62.909	23.486	59.6	
1980	194.944	132.035	209.9	6
1990	280.297	85.353	43.8	
2000	621.627	341.330	121.8	7
2009	1,964.319	1,342.692	216.0	7
2014	4,100.000	1,894.319	96.4	7
2016	3,833.000	- 267.000	- 6.5	
2-2017	3,763.907	- 69,093	- 1.8	

Notes for Table 1:
a) Info:
1. Data from Federal Reserve Bank-St.Louis in Billion USD
http://research.stlouisfed.org/fred2/series/AMBNS, to Feb-2017.
2. 'M0' is basic currency supply (notes and coins),
b) Analysis of Table Data:
3. The Federal Reserve System started in 1913; Fed did large M0 increase in '30s to help England after WW1,
4. Fed reduced M0 quickly due to market frenzy in late '30s, a major cause of the depression,
5. Fed increased M0 to fund WW2,
6. Fed increased M0 in '80s as a stimulant after the '80-81' recession, which led to the dot.com bubble in '90s,
 7. Fed increased M0 in 1999 to 2006 to recover from the dot.com bubble. This became the underlying cause of the 2007 housing bubble burst as it fed the CRA, Fannie, Freddie, Ginnie Mae, and Main Street and Wall Street binges of excessive spending and credit. The QE-1 'Bernanke Spike' of $2 trill. in late 2008 was to stimulate the economy after the housing bubble burst in 2007. Then QE-2, and in Sep-2012 QE-3 spending $40 bn per mo. on mortgage-based securities, plus the existing 'Operation Twist' of $45 bn mo. QE ended in Oct-2014.

****

The Fed reduces the value of our money by excessive expansion of money supply (create new money, 'monetary inflation'). Proof is shown in the start and end "purchase power" amounts below are from www.measuringworth.com.

It took **$1,202.05** in the year 1912 for the same "purchase power" as **$1,000** in the year **1774 (a 17.7% loss in 138 yrs**, or 0.13 % per yr).

It took **$22,427.40** in the year 2008 for the same "purchase power" as **$1,000** in the year 1913 **(a 95.5% loss in 95 yrs**). Almost eight times more than before the Fed!

In Table 1, notice the large 'dollar' increase from 2000 to 2009, which contributed to the bubble that burst in 2008. A decline in purchasing power of the dollar follows this increase in the money supply. The Dollar lost 95% of its value from 1913 (when the Fed started) to 2000, but 80% of that loss occurred after Nixon cut the Bretton Woods tie to gold in 1971, and the money supply increased faster.

The main purpose of convertibility of paper (or electronic dollars) to gold is to prevent excessive expansion of the money supply (monetary 'inflation') by the government, and thus reduction in purchasing power. Without convertibility, this 'easy money' is an unlimited 'piggy-bank' and credit card for the government.
. This unlimited supply of money has allowed massive increases in government spending and debt for wars, welfare, and pork since 1971. It has also created the growth in the number of lobbyists seeking favors.

Table 2
The Honest National Debt and Unfunded Liabilities

A. $ 19.9 tn National Debt (disclosed debt)

B.	105.5	Misc. unfunded Liabilities ('off- budget')
	27.7	Medicare A, B, and D (unfunded)
	15.8	Social Security (unfunded)

$ 149.0 trillion   Total for B

$ 168.9 trillion = Grand Total (A+B)

(Source: USDebtClock.org, Mar. 16, 2017)

Notes: 1) Liabilities are unfunded promises based on current tax and funding inputs, various assumptions, and future demographic shifts in U.S. population, 2) National (public) debt is the total of; a. the face or principal amount of all securities (marketable and unmarketable – owned by Fed -)

currently outstanding, b. military and civilian pensions, c. retiree health benefits, and d. other guarantees and obligations.

The 'official' government debt figures ignore the above Medicare, Soc. Sec. and Misc. items (treated as 'off-budget' !!), plus potential trillions that loom due to losses at Fannie and Freddie, now government-owned.

In 1970 the national debt was $380.9 bill. (about $3.4 tn in 2012 dollars), and 37.6% of GDP. As of Mar-2017, national debt was $19.9 trill. and 1065.2% of the $18.9 tn GDP! (**www.usgovernmentspending.com**, and USDebtClock.org) All economists agree that debt over 100% of GDP is dangerous! No one believes the debt will ever be paid! Overt default (refusal to pay; repudiation) of most of it is one strategy. Another is creating new fake money (the IMF 'SDR'?; see p. 134), but this would likely cause hyper price inflation, and destroy the US Dollar and economy. Horrible choices, and all thanks to irresponsible government leaders.
Of course consumer (personal) debt (cars, home mortgages – first and second -, credit cards, TVs, etc.) zoomed upward because of the easy (lax terms, subprime), cheap (low interest) fake money created by the Fed in 2000 to 2007, and is now about $17.9 tn ! As more people lose their jobs, more bills go unpaid, and the defaults and foreclosures are now doing the upward zoom. Sad.

The government is broke, yet the 'political' spending persists! Governors and Congresspersons seek Federal money for all manner of State projects, but it comes with strings attached, which lets the DC folks control many aspects of State functions (Bye-Bye to States' Rights).

Prices started their 'hockey stick' shaped rise a few years after Nixon severed the Dollar's ties to gold in Aug -1971 as the effect of excess money and spending trickled to the world economy. Within in a few years, all nations worldwide ceased convertibility, even the prudent Swiss floated the Swiss Franc (CHF), but have been less abusive than others; hence while 1 USD=about 4 CHF in 1961, it is now about 1 US=1 sf, so they only inflated by 2.5 while by 2008 the US inflated by 10; 4 times more! The USA has been the worst abuser among developed nations (older countries remembered their lessons from past monetary failures). The US has created so much new 'free, fake money' since 1971 that the USD has lost about 80% of its purchasing power (this excess expansion of the money supply is called 'inflation', like a balloon) with its consequent price increases. Check prices of common 'commodity' items that are not imported, subsidized, cheaper due to new technology, or under price control, such as a pizza, or a restaurant meal.

A good example is that a room at 'Motel 6' cost $6 in the '50s and is now in the $60 range in 2008 (same type of room and service). There is your 10X loss of USD value! This goes along with a 95% loss since the Federal Reserve monopoly was created in 1913! The only reason we can get away with this is because the USD is the world's 'reserve currency' (any person or bank will accept it as payment, and keep it as if 'good as gold'), because it is viewed as a share in 'USA, Inc.', the world's strongest economy, which sadly is fading. The era of USA world dominance is ending.

What is the solution? Our "Rebuild America' plan in Chapter 5 offers key changes in laws, policies, and spending. This is a massive project, but if we don't start soon, the USD will crash in value (by 50% or more) as people, merchants, and governments worldwide reject it.

To those who join us in the fight for more liberty and personal responsibility, I say '**Thanks, we must never give up.**'

Chapter 4: Key Issues

All of the issues discussed below are part of the 'Rebuild America' plan, as discussed further in Chapter 5. We comment on 33 topics below, but we will add and delete as needed. Send suggestions and comments to me at **RedickD@AOL.com**, and see updates at **Forward-USA.org** (part 3 in the left margin). Thanks.

I will add comparisons to the Trump Solution (if documented) for each issue below. This will evolve as things happen. If we disagree with Pres. Trump, we will submit a constructive, polite, suggestion.

Most of the statements below are lengthy in order to be complete. However, if you just read the first 10 or 15 lines, you will have read the main points. Where you see 'Our Position' (or 'Solution') below, it means the 'Forward USA" recommendation.

Contents of Chapter 4:

Issue

For information on other issues, please contact Dave at **RedickD@AOl.com**. I appreciate your interest.

****

1. The Constitution:

We have observed many examples of people (including some in government who should know better) treating the Constitution as a set of laws and rules that control citizens. Wrong! The purpose of the Constitution is to define what the government must, may, and may not do, by making it a short list of 'enumerated powers'. Congress (the Legislature) makes the laws! That's one of the reasons the 18th amendment (alcohol prohibition) was wrong, it put restrictions on the people. The same applies to a proposed amendment for abortion. Such issues should be passed as laws at the state level, or not at all (if unconstitutional, or none of the government's business, as is true of most things). It is the job of us citizens, and our elected 'leaders', to maintain those limits and keep the government (at ALL levels) on a short leash. The intent was, 'if it is not on the list, the government can't do it!' Many Founders, led by George Mason, balked even at this restraint. They didn't trust the government (and its power-seeking elected members) to stay within the limits, so they wouldn't support ratification until a 'Bill of Rights' (the first ten amendments) to protect the rights of the people and States was included. They were right! The Constitution has been abused to gain power for Federal politicians and their friends. Today, more than half of laws and spending are unconstitutional. Abuse of the 'implied powers', 'general welfare', and 'interstate commerce' provisions account for most deviations. A further misunderstanding is that we are a Democracy. Wrong. In a Democracy the citizens vote directly to make laws, and **tyranny of the majority soon rules.** We are a Constitutional Republic, where we vote for Representatives who in turn are restricted by the Constitution.

A 'short leash' is required on government power at all levels (city, county, state, federal) because we grant them 'police powers' (legal use of force by police and military) which is easily abused. The current 'War on Terror' and 'Patriot Act' are good examples of abuse.

2. Our Core Principle:

Most elected officials take positions based on their feelings, personal preferences, and pressure from the special interest groups who give them money or votes. All 'Forward USA' positions are based on an **objective principle,** which is:

"The proper role of government is to PROTECT the personal and property rights of its citizens, as INDIVIDUALS, from violation or threat by OTHERS."

With this approach, government ownership and control is minimized, and human interaction is more peaceful and voluntary (it pays to get along!), and has a proven track record of producing more liberty, peace, prosperity, morality, and justice, **proportional to the extent it is employed.**

If so, why do people support 'more-government' systems known as **Progressive, Liberal, or Socialist?** The key is they hope to fund their projects with 'other people's money' by 'tax the rich' schemes. **While popular (most people like to have others pay for their benefits), these systems use inherently immoral and coercive 'gang theft by vote' taxation, which results in declining peace, productivity, and justice, if you count all the side-effects** (including robbing 'the rich' by forced payment of their so-called 'fair share'). Liberals-Progressives purposely ignore that the top 10 percent of income earners pay about 70 percent of all federal income taxes though they earn only 43 percent of all income. Isn't that enough?? The bottom 50 percent pay only 2 percent of income taxes but earn 13 percent of total income. About half of tax filers paid no federal income tax at all. Note it is 'dollars' that count, not 'percentages'!
A society that broadly accepts this type of immoral funding is in decline, as shown by falling morality in all parts of US activity since the 1950s. Sad!

Key points to understanding and using our Core Principle are:

a) Our Federal and State governments were created by, and are still controlled by, 'we the people' to protect our rights (a short list of 'natural rights' you are born with, which does not include subsidized or free health care, education, etc.). Thus, the government is our servant, not our owner, manager, funder, or nanny. To implement this protection (enforce the laws), we grant the government 'police powers' (the right to use force), and thus we need to be ever on guard to avoid abuse, including use of laws beyond their intended purpose (RICO, FISA, etc.). For individuals, the flip side of this is; "A person should never initiate force except in self-defense", or " Persons can do whatever they want to, short of violating the equal rights of others". In a personal (not legal) context, I suggest that each person has a moral obligation to be a beneficial presence in the world, and not offensive to others. This starts with being honest, kind, courteous and clean.

Personal rights are freedom of religion, speech, etc. Some of these are listed in the Constitution, but in fact all are 'natural' at birth, and not bestowed by the government (which can only protect or abuse them; not create, except for contrived 'legislated' rights). Our Founders debated if any should be listed (to avoid exclusion of some not listed), hence they included Amendment IX. Note that only a human individual has personal rights.

Notice that 1. Words like 'manage our money, social system, and economy', 'mother', and 'police the world' are not included in the Principle, and 2. We are not 'created equal' as to mind, body and circumstances, but all citizens have equal rights under the law.

Property includes tangibles, and intellectual property owned by a person or legal organization (corporation, etc.). Except for government restrictions (often unconstitutional), a property right is; " The right to use and dispose of your property (use, sell, loan, lease, give, etc.) however you see fit, short of violating the equal rights of others."

Property rights need to be treated as superior to personal rights in order to avoid conflicts. For example, if you enter someone's property without permission (trespassing) and start to give a sermon, your freedom of speech and religion are not being violated if you are made to leave.

b) The government needs police, courts, and military for national DEFENSE to do its job, all used within the limits of the Constitution. But note that the military must not be used to enforce or solve political or economic issues abroad, when there is no threat to our homeland (such as the Vietnam, Iraq, Afghan and Libyan wars).

c) There are no group rights (by sex, race, age, etc.). Every citizen has the same rights. We should not create 'preferred minorities' with special privileges, which are easily abused. There should be no subjective versions of laws, such as a 'Hate Crimes'. Theft is theft, murder, is murder.

d) Nothing can be a right if you expect someone else to pay for even part of it (such as health, education, etc.). Insurance is a method to share risks and expenses, but must be voluntary, or if run as a 'single payer' by the government, have equal benefits to all, based on terms and payments, and not include a 'welfare' aspect where some members pay less for the same coverage. For example, using property tax to pay for public schools is a rip-off of owners since there is no connection to whether the payer has kids in school (but it is convenient politically!).

e) Your body is your property. If you hurt yourself, or put yourself at risk, it is none of the government's business. Note that the Core principle above ends in 'by others'.

f) The same principle of 'protection' applies to the property rights of business and other legal entities.

g) As with people, the government has no authorization to be the 'owner, manager, funder, or nanny' of the 'national economy'. Free enterprise does a great job of supplying goods and services, while government interference (controls, subsidies, etc.) always do more harm than good, if all the side-effects (including inflation and depressions) are counted.

h) Provision of 'essential services' conflicts with the principle of only 'protecting rights', and is a constant threat to limiting the size of government at all levels (city, county, state, and federal). This is where the federal 'General Welfare' clause is most abused. While most should be 'privatized', to the extent these projects (such as education, sewer, water, roads, public health, parks, mass transit, etc.) are unfortunately approved, they should at least be;
  1. Charged to users at compensatory rates (user fees, tuition, no subsidies). Again, voluntary private charity can help the truly needy.
  2. Built and operated by contractors on a competitive-bid basis. . The main reason the Federal government has become huge, and involved in running or financing so many unconstitutional state and city projects, is that unlike the States and cities, it never runs out of money, thanks to the Federal Reserve piggy-bank of fake money!

i) The above Core Principle refers to 'violation or threat by OTHERS'. The government only has a role to act when such violations or threats are imposed on someone, and they have no choice to avoid it. For example, non-smokers can avoid privately-owned places that allow smoking (bars, etc; just don't go there!), so it would be a violation of the owner's property rights to impose a non-smoking ordinance, but not City Hall (there is only one, and there are times when you are required to go there; no choice), or other government sites. However, while it is improper to use the legal system to impose your personal preferences on others (smoking, religion, zoning, etc.), there is the viable alternative of 'voluntary negotiation.' This means you (or a group you form) approach the bar owners, or your neighbors, and try to make a deal that serves your wants and needs. Bar owners want customers; maybe they will create a non-smoking room. This applies to any situation. It is peaceful and proper, and no 'tyranny of the majority' is employed.

j) The government cannot do things that are illegal or immoral if done by citizens. Sadly, unethical practices (which should be illegal) such as 'progressive' taxation ('tax the rich' at a higher rate) are justified as 'needed' and a method of charging 'fair share', while in fact it is simply 'gang-theft-by-vote'. Why not have the government rob banks, or give guns to the Red Cross and United Way, for fund raising? This violation of rights is 'tyranny of the majority' and cannot be justified because it is 'the will of the people', 'the American way', and done by the government. There are many other examples (military draft, subsidies, legislative favors, etc.).

The maze of 'social engineering' laws that tell us how to live and work do much more harm than good when all the side effects (unintended consequences) are considered. My approach emphasizes liberty, personal responsibility, and limited government, which is consistent with our American heritage and Constitution, and history shows it results in maximum liberty, peace, prosperity, ethics, and justice.
Look at the conditions in countries around the world with 'big government' (Progressive, Socialism, or Dictatorships) and judge for yourself. Start with N. Korea, Cuba, and the several 'xxstans' (former Soviet Republics).

3. Debt, Taxes and Spending:

See the plan in Chapter 5 for more details.

A. Debt: Domestic and foreign debts are at record levels, for both persons and businesses. With a 'national' (or 'public') debt of over $16 trillion, the U.S. government is the world's biggest debtor (and this doesn't count the over $181 trillions of unfunded Social Security and Medicare obligations, P.49). Former Chairman Greenspan of the Federal Reserve Bank (Fed) kept interest rates artificially low (not market-driven) from 2000 to 2006 so mortgages were cheap, to 'stimulate' the economy. It is just like taking heroin, and has withdrawal pains when the economy gets 'sick' from mal-investment (too much money chasing deals). People and business borrowed and spent too much of this cheap money, and then the Fed changed policy, so in 2008 we got; 1. A credit 'crunch' (banks have less money to loan), and 2. Increased interest rates that drove-up ARM (adjustable rate) mortgages. This is what caused foreclosures as home 'owners' couldn't meet their increased payments. Alan Greenspan (Fed Chm. from 1987 to 2006) knew he was creating this monster, but did it to keep his job by pleasing his political bosses. I say he should be indicted for malfeasance and fraud! Instead, he is treated like a sage by his accomplices in Congress and Think Tanks. Ben Bernanke (Fed Chm. from 2006 to present) has used 'Quantitative Easing' (Fed-speak for flooding the economy with new money) called QE-1, 2, and 3-Forever as a 'stimulus', but as any Austrian (see Glossary, P. 177) economist would predict, it isn't working!

Much of the money we send abroad to buy imports comes back to buy government debt or U.S. assets (Treasury Notes, T-Bills, golf courses, businesses, etc.), but that won't go on forever because investors know **the US Dollar (USD) is at risk of collapse due to excess creation of new money by the Fed (called 'monetary inflation', an increase in the money supply, like a balloon; which reduces the purchasing power of all USD).**

B. Taxes: Taxes divert money to the government so people and firms can't use it to spend or invest. History shows that the government uses it unwisely, so the economy and standard of living suffer. We must reduce taxes and spending of all types, and abolish most taxes. **I say start by cutting tax rates by 50% or more (the Laffer Curve says revenues might drop less).** We recommend 'user fees' (school tuition, toll roads, some 'public services', etc.) whenever feasible, and a 'sales' tax (Not a 'Value Added Tax, VAT, which hides the layers involved) to replace the 'Big Six' of income (personal and corporate), property, interest, capital gains, and inheritance taxes. All of these six taxes amount to a 'penalty on success' and targeted gang-theft, plus a double-tax for inheritance. The sales tax is non-intrusive to personal affairs, less 'progressive' (zero or less 'penalty on success'; except that big spenders pay more), has no disincentive to work and earn, and is easy to manage. Again, Liberals/Progressives like to tax 'the rich' to make them pay their 'fair share', but purposely ignore that the top 10 percent of income earners pay about 70 percent of all federal income taxes though they earn only 43 percent of all income. Isn't that enough??

C. Spending

The U.S. economy and dollar are in trouble, and while our DC 'Leaders' are very worried about it, but won't admit it to us regular folks. They start wars to gain control of oil and other nations instead.

. **Federal spending is out of control.** All the elected folks in DC are on a 'feel-good', 'vote-for-me' binge of unconstitutional and excess projects including wars, empire building, pork-barrel earmarks, and projects that should be handled by States, or eliminated. I say; 'Cut spending by at least 50%.

4. 9/11 and the War on Terror

The facts and logic (means and motive) related to the 9/11 tragedy build a strong case that it was planned by USA for the forever 'War on Terror' and our invasions of Afghanistan and Iraq (for starters).

Never forget that; 1) We claim 15 of the 19 bombers who planned and executed 9/11 were Saudis, and 2) A group of Saudi Royals were allowed to fly out of the US on Sep. 12 even though there was a stop on all flights. **Why didn't we invade Saudi Arabia and do a 'regime change' on the despotic royal family? (Hint: We already had a good oil deal with them).** The Saudi Royals, old family friends of the Bushes, are hated by their people, and have paid-off their dominant Wahhabi clerics (a militant sect of Islam and operators of radical anti-American/Christian/Jew mosques and Madrasah schools worldwide; these are the guys who like to lash women because they have been raped) with oil money over the years to avoid a revolution. **Ignoring Saudi Arabia is your first clue that Bush and his team had a hidden agenda for the War on Terror!**

Many well informed, well educated, and sincere people have concluded that **the government at least 'facilitated' the 9/11 attack** as a 'trigger' for their plans to invade Iraq and expand 'Empire-USA'. Israeli and DC both wanted an excuse to invade Iraq and Iran. How else does one explain the series of events such as; 1) FBI inputs on pilot training by Arabs were ignored, 2) NORAD planes were not launched, 3) The towers and building 7 fell straight down at free-fall speed (this can only happen by controlled demolition !), plus the towers were a 'tube' design with large vertical exterior I-beams as the main structure. These beams were cut (severed!) at each floor as the towers fell; HOW?? No body-parts or furniture were in the rubble, WHY? (they were pulverized!), 4) A demolition company was at the tower site the next morning to haul away debris to a restricted site, then ship it overseas for scrap. (this prevented analysis of how the tower exterior I-beams were cut, and was a massive violation of the crime scene), and 5) the debris and damage at the Pentagon were more consistent with a ground-launched missile than an airliner crash, and videos of the crash and debris were locked-up. The list of suspicious events goes on and on. A further dimension is that the WTC owner, L. Silverstein, faced a huge expense in ridding the towers of asbestos, and had put a big insurance policy on the buildings, with an extra-cost terrorist clause. For more info, see **www.scholarsfor9/11truth.org**, and Dr. Paul Craig Roberts Sep-2011 article: **www.globalresearch.ca/index.php?context=va&aid=26520** . The case is not closed!! The 'official' 9/11 report is full of errors, bias, poor research, and voids. Calling the citizen investigators 'kooks' working on 'conspiracy theories' will not stop discovery of the truth. **This contrived justification for the disastrous War on Terror must be exposed so that the War can be stopped.**

 If you find it hard to believe that our leaders would lie to start a war, and allow our troops to be killed and maimed for political and economic reasons (not for defense), then review my column **'Wars, and The Lies that Start Them'** (published on Sep-2007) in Appendix 1.

The Bush team of 'neocons' (former Liberals such as Wolfowitz, Perle, Kristol, Abrams, and Feith who became 'new conservatives' to seek their personal goals; for more information reference the article **"My Alma Mater is a Moral Cesspool"** on the Counterpunch.org website) took advantage of the atmosphere of crisis generated by 9/11 to create the 'War on Terror' as a general-purpose, and forever, project to implement their plan to use force to gain control of oil and politics worldwide. The result has been an immoral, illegal and counterproductive crusade.

. The documented information below traces how Bush and his team got us into this mess and why it will be costly, or impossible, to correct it. All information is verifiable from multiple sources.

The purpose of Clinton's Balkans war was; 1. To gain control of the Balkans region so we could build oil pipelines through it, 2. Build huge Camp Bondsteel as a regional supply center and airbase, and 3. To evict China from Eastern Europe and its oil, including the Caspian area. Remember the 'accidental' bombing of the Chinese embassy in Belgrade? Why was NATO involved when no NATO member had been attacked? **Bush's invasion and occupation of Afghanistan was primarily to get access to build an oil/gas pipeline** from Turkmenistan and Uzbekistan to a warm water port near Karachi, Pakistan (the same reason the Russians invaded in the 1980's; Google 'Afghanistan, Unocal'). This project had been delayed for many years but was suddenly approved in Dec-2001.

On June 22, 2008, Eric Margolis, Mid East expert, and former Toronto Sun journalist (ericmargolis.com), issued the article: **'These wars are about Oil, not Democracy'** which tied together the various political, economic, and oil/gas issues as follows (excerpts): *"PARIS -- The ugly truth behind the Iraq and Afghanistan wars finally has emerged. Four major western oil companies, Exxon Mobil, Shell, BP and Total are about to sign U.S.-brokered no-bid contracts to begin exploiting Iraq's oil fields. Saddam Hussein had kicked these firms out three decades ago when he nationalized Iraq's oil industry. The U.S.-installed Baghdad regime is welcoming them back. Iraq is getting back the same oil companies that used to exploit it when it was a British colony.*

As former Fed chairman Alan Greenspan recently admitted, the Iraq war was all about oil. The invasion was about SUV's, not democracy.

Afghanistan just signed a major deal to launch a long-planned, 1,680-km pipeline project expected to cost $8 billion. If completed, the Turkmenistan-Afghanistan-Pakistan-India pipeline (TAPI) will export gas and later oil from the Caspian basin (Turkmenistan) to Pakistan's Arabian Sea coast where tankers will transport it to the West.

The Caspian basin located under the Central Asian states of Turkmenistan, Uzbekistan and Kazakkstan, holds an estimated 300 trillion cubic feet of gas and 100-200 billion barrels of oil. Securing the world's last remaining known energy El Dorado is a strategic priority for the western powers.

But there are only two practical ways to get gas and oil out of land-locked Central Asia to the sea: Through Iran, or through Afghanistan to Pakistan. Iran is taboo for Washington. That leaves Pakistan, but to get there, the planned pipeline must cross western Afghanistan, including the cities of Herat and Kandahar.

PIPELINE DEAL: In 1998, the Afghan anti-Communist movement Taliban and a western oil consortium led by the U.S. firm Unocal signed a major pipeline deal. Unocal lavished money and attention on the Taliban, flew a senior delegation to Texas, and hired a minor Afghan official, Hamid Karzai.

Enter Osama bin Laden. He advised the unworldly Taliban leaders to reject the U.S. deal and got them to accept a better offer from an Argentine consortium. Washington was furious and, according to some accounts, threatened the Taliban with war. **In early 2001, six or seven months before 9/11, Washington made the decision to invade Afghanistan, overthrow the Taliban, and install a client regime that would build the energy pipelines**. But Washington still kept sending money to the Taliban until four months before 9/11 in an effort to keep it "on side" for possible use in a war against China.

The 9/11 attacks, about which the Taliban knew nothing, supplied the pretext to invade Afghanistan. The initial U.S. operation had the legitimate objective of wiping out Osama bin Laden's al-Qaida. But after its 300 members fled to Pakistan, the U.S. stayed on, built bases -- which just happened to be adjacent to the planned pipeline route -- and installed former Unocal "consultant" Hamid Karzai as leader.

Washington disguised its energy geopolitics by claiming the Afghan occupation was to fight "Islamic terrorism," liberate women, build schools and promote democracy. Ironically, the Soviets made exactly the same claims when they occupied Afghanistan from 1979-1989. The Iraq cover story was weapons of mass destruction and democracy.

Work will begin on the TAPI once Taliban forces are cleared from the pipeline route by U.S., Canadian and NATO forces. As American analyst Kevin Phillips writes, the U.S. military and its allies have become an "energy protection force."

Margolis also gave us early warning with his March 2, 2003 article '**Bush's War is Not About Democracy**', which said, in part: *"Bush's war is not about democracy, weapons of mass destruction, human rights, or terrorism. It has two main motivations. First, the Manifest Destiny crowd in Washington, led by VP Dick Cheney and Defense Secretary Donald Rumsfeld. The terrible events of 9/11 have seemed to produce an almost psychotic reaction in these good, patriotic Americans, transforming them into 19th century imperialists.*

Their intention is perfectly clear: 1) prevent any nation ever challenging U.S. global hegemony; 2) dominate oil. The aggression against Iraq is not about oil per se, it is about control of oil. Before the Iraq crisis, the U.S. imported about $18 billion of crude oil annually from the Mideast, but spent $31 billion keeping military forces there. Why? Control of Mideast oil gives the U.S. domination over Europe and Japan, which draw most of their oil from the region.

Domination of the Mideast and Caspian Sea oil will assure the U.S. a stranglehold over China, India, and Europe.

The second driving force is Israel's far-right Likud government, many of whose ideas have come to dominate Bush admin. policy and U.S. media on the Mideast.

The Clinton administration was close to Israel's moderate Labour Party; Bush's camp is totally aligned with Israel's aggressive far right and mirrors its views and policies to a remarkable, unprecedented degree.

Likud and its powerful American supporters want the U.S. to crush Iraq into pieces. **The principal beneficiary of the war against Iraq will be Israel.**

ADDED BENEFIT: From Washington's viewpoint, the TAPI deal has the added benefit of scuttling another proposed pipeline project that would have delivered Iranian gas and oil to Pakistan and India.

India's energy needs are expected to triple over the next decade. Delhi, which has its own designs on Afghanistan, is cock-a-hoop over the new pipeline plan.
Russia, by contrast, is grumpy, having hoped to monopolize Central Asian energy exports.

Energy is more important than blood in our modern world. The U.S. is a great power with massive energy needs. Domination of oil is a pillar of America's world power. Let's be realistic. Afghanistan and Iraq are about oil, nothing else."

Too bad the US citizens and Congress didn't pay more attention to Margolis' prescient words.
On May 13, 2009, Pepe Escobar wrote a fine piece tying together all the pipeline activity and war-politics in the greater Mid east with his: **'Pipeline-Istan: Everything You Need to Know About Oil, Gas, Russia, China, Iran, Afghanistan and Obama'** (see **www.alternet.org/story/139983**). It shows

how oil dominates all the major military and political activity there, including the USA invasions and wars in Iraq and Afghanistan. **This again confirms that the War on Terror is mostly a false-front to justify invading and controlling greater Mid East countries (from the xxstans to N. Africa; Libya, Mali next?) to get their oil.**

Iraq never threatened the US and Saddam was not a cohort of Osama. As stated by former US Treasurer Paul O'Neill, **Bush and his team had been planning to invade Iraq well before 9/11.** Bush fired him for his lack of 'loyalty', as discussed in O'neill's book 'The Price of Loyalty'. For further insight on Iraq, visit the '**A War in Search of a Reason**' column by Ivan Eland. Thus, they started building a case for preemptive war by fabricating phony reasons such as WMDs and branded Iraq as a part of 9/11.

In his 'Letter to the American People' in Nov-2002 (see guardian.co.uk/world/2002/nov/24/theobserver), Osama bin Laden stated that his reasons for opposing the USA were; 1) US bases in Saudi Arabia, 2) extreme US support of Israel, 3) bombing of Iraq for ten years, since 1991, and 4) support of the corrupt Saudi royal family and sale of oil at low prices, denominated only in US dollars (Petrodollars, a deal made by FDR in 1945, and Nixon in 1973). Here is the Sept. 28, 2001 interview in which bin Laden states his was not involved with the 9/11 attack; ummatpublication.com/2012/11/25/). As shown in the Margolis quote starting on P. 51 above, Osama was our 'friend' until in 1999 he helped Argentina get the pipeline deal through Afghanistan, so became our enemy! By early 2011 we had decided to invade Afghanistan and 'take' the pipeline deal. Hence our quick invasion on Oct. 7, 2001, 26 days after 9/11 ! Such a major military action required many months of planning!

A study done by Prof. W. Pape at the University of Chicago, and part of his book 'Dying to Win', shows that **the primary reason driving suicide terrorists is opposition to occupying troops in their homeland** (not religion), which we had done for many years in Saudi Arabia. Yet Bush pushes the fabrication that 'they hate our way of life' as a diversion from the truth. On Dec. 30, 2005 Dr. Paul Craig Roberts, Assistant Secretary of Treasury under Reagan, wrote, *"Bush claims that his war crimes are justified because they are committed in the name of 'freedom and democracy'. The entire world rejects this excuse. Sooner or later even Bush's remaining Republican supporters will turn away in shame from the dishonor Bush has brought to America."* On Jan. 16, 2006, in his excellent essay on how our Executive branch is becoming dictatorial (**http://www.lewrockwell.com/roberts/roberts139.html**), Dr. Roberts wrote, *" It is paradoxical that American democracy is the likely casualty of a "war on terror" that is being justified in the name of the expansion of democracy."*

The **TRUE REASONS Bush invaded Iraq are**:
1) Control of oil (a step to control the greater Mid East),
2) Defense of Israel (plus access to water, oil, and more land for them),
3) Land for permanent bases (hence they had no 'exit strategy'; we built a huge embassy, plus four large airbases and many smaller ones), and
4) Defense of the U.S. dollar (Saddam had converted to selling oil in Euros; we reversed that the day after our invasion).

Also, the Christian Right has a religious reason for insuring the special treatment of Israel, since they believe Israel must exist in order to allow the second coming of Christ. Faith-based persons of influence who under Bush favored special treatment of Israel in US policy were led by Tom DeLay, and John Ashcroft, now add Lindsey Graham, and most Jewish House and Senate persons.

In Jan-2006 the sabers started rattling to justify bombing Iran, and are getting louder today in Jan-2013. The 'official' reasons may be different, but the Real Reasons will be the same as three of the above for IRAQ (oil, Israel and defense of the US Dollar). Iran has announced plans to sell oil in Euros. Israel bought 100 'bunker-buster' bombs from us in Nov-2004 (just after the election), and is ready to use them.

The vast 'War on Terror' was created primarily as a cover to give U.S. empire builders the authority to increase their control by meddling in the affairs of other nations worldwide (which just creates new enemies), and restrict objections at home. The 'USA Patriot Act' gives the government excess authority, which is easily abused. Under it, even US citizens tend to be viewed by authorities as 'guilty until proven innocent', and are at risk of being secretly spied upon, or arrested, as terror suspects if they criticize government conduct and policies. All these programs continue with no end, or net benefit, in sight.

A better solution is to stop interfering in the internal affairs of other nations so that we don't create enemies. As noted above, the primary cause of suicide terrorist attacks is the presence of occupying troops. We should withdraw from our immoral, illegal, and counterproductive ventures in Afghan and Iraq, and most of our bases in over 130 countries worldwide. Bush and his team don't want to withdraw from anywhere because they want to control these places, thus control more oil (and deny it to China), and continue building an Empire worldwide. **I believe in strong defense, but not costly and useless wars that can be avoided with no harm to us (Not for defense).**

5. How Oil, War, 9/11, and the US Dollar are Tied

There is a cause-and-effect connection between oil, value of the US Dollar, and 9/11. The two huge problems, shown in A. and B. below, were known by the Bush Team when they entered office in Jan-2001. They had a warfare plan to control oil and politics worldwide, but 9/11 gave them cover to get started sooner and bigger.

A. Risk of Collapse of the U.S. Dollar (USD): The value of the USD is now propped-up in part by the fact that most oil sales (to any buyer) are denominated in the USD. The market value (purchasing power) of all fiat currencies (just paper; no gold or silver content or redeemability) depends on the willingness of others to **use it** (market demand), and **hold it** as savings, or for a nation, as foreign exchange reserves (typically in the form of US government bonds). All transactions are part of demand, but oil purchases are one of the largest and most visible. A major shift to use of another currency, such as the Euro, would cause a drop in USD value, and could trigger a panic to get rid of USD holdings (cash, bonds, real estate) by foreign persons and nations to avoid major loss of value (30 to 50 percent, or more). China has already started, and S. Korea has hinted. Japan could be next. These three countries are the biggest holders of USD denominated assets. A USD collapse would cause a major US depression, and affect others worldwide.

A shift to the Euro (or any other non-USD currency or gold) by other countries for; 1) Oil purchases, 2) Investments (bonds, businesses anywhere, etc.), or 3) Foreign currency reserves, would reduce support for the USD and is a nightmare scenario for the US.
In Nov-2002 Saddam converted to Euros, which we reversed just after the Mar-2003 invasion. Venezuela is threatening to convert. Iran started its own 'Bourse' trading exchange in early 2007, and trades in multiple currencies, including the USD, Euro, and Yen. The shift to Euros puts these countries on top of the list for intervention by the US. The CIA plot to unseat Venezuela's Pres. Chavez in Apr-2002 didn't work, but he was on notice. His death on March 5, 2013 starts a new strategy!

Our Solution: The USD is vulnerable because of; 1) Excessive expansion of the money supply ('Inflation', to

pay government bills), and 2) **Excess spending and debt by the government. Reversal of these errors will bring strength.**

B. Loss of Oil and Gas Control to Russia, China and India: The oil industry agrees that within about 20 years the earth will reach 'peak oil' production. This means the wells for cheap oil (easy to reach, pump, and refine) will start producing less ('peak oil'). There will be lots of oil left (tar sands, shale 'fracking', etc.), but it will be very expensive to acquire and refine. The US is competing with other countries (mostly China and India; Russia has its own) for control of the remaining cheap oil. They are traveling the world together to negotiate long term contracts (China announced one with Saudi Arabia in Jan-2006). The U.S. is invading oil producers on false pretenses to gain control. Russia's long dispute/war in Chechnya is mostly about control of oil, gas, and pipelines in the Caspian region where Russia seeks broad control. India and China face oil shortages in the future so they are cooperating in deals to gain control of oil in the MidEast, Africa and SE Asia. This threatens US availability and price of over 80% of the world's proven 'cheap' reserves. **These are key reasons for the US wars in the Balkans, Afghanistan, and Iraq, and threats to Iran**. The stakes could not be higher, including risk of broad and long wars, and economic depression, for all nations involved.

Rather than seeking military and political control of oil-producing nations (a costly and immoral method), the US should negotiate long-term contracts for supply. Big customers have clout! This approach will also end creating enemies by meddling in the affairs of other countries.
With the Iraq war not going well, Bush collaborated with the former enemy Sunnis (Cheney's Jan-2006 trip around the region) on a deal to reduce the anti-US attacks inside Iraq so the US can declare victory and get out 'with honor'. **Of course the original plan was to stay forever in order to; a) Control**

Iraq oil, b) Use permanent bases in Iraq to control the Mid East, c) Defend Israel, and d) Keep Iraq oil sales in US Dollars.

Bush's failure to capture Osama bin Laden was no accident. Having him at large helped keep him (and now Obama) as 'War Presidents' so the above issues could be pursued as part of the forever War on Terror. The same applies to onerous checking and restrictions by the TSA on carry-on luggage for air travel, while the checked baggage is barely inspected. This keeps 'the people' on edge about terror, so they will not object to loss of liberties. The illegal and desperate measures (domestic spying, torture, etc.) taken by Bush showed his concern about avoiding new attacks on US soil, which are made even more likely by his ongoing intervention for the above issues in the Mid East.

FLASH - The so-called 'Killing of Osama' in May-2011 by a Navy Seal raid was a staged event to boost Obama's popularity. All insiders believe he died from kidney disease years before. The ultra-phony picture of Hillary, Gates and others watching the raid on TV was a bad joke. The quick dumping of the body at sea, and the convenient death of all the Seals in a later accident??, are two of the many other well-documented reasons to show the whole event was fake.

I support a strong defense, and wars entered for valid reasons approved by Congress. **In their effort to solve the above problems and gain power worldwide, I say the Bush Team operated as an Imperial Presidency, with excess use of force and secrecy, which conflicts with stated USA and Republican principles.** They are using: 1) foreign aid, intervention, and war in a plan to control the world's politics and oil, and 2) high spending, funded by debt, to pacify the folks at home. The first version of the warfare plan was secretly issued in Sep-2000 by the 'Project for a New American Century' team (PNAC, a DC think tank) which started in 1997. The plan called for increased military force worldwide to promote control of oil and their special-interest politics. When Bush was elected in Nov-2000, many of the authors (including Rumsfeld, Perle, Kagan, Feith, Abrams, and Wolfowitz: Cheney was a cofounder) joined the Bush team. For details, refer to the 25Feb03 essay, '**The Project for the New American Century**', by William Pitt and Scott Ritter (former UN Inspector for Iraq weapons). **As shown by the demise of all previous empires in history, this approach never works. It is a path to military, economic, and ethical failure**. Perhaps due to the bad reputation they got from the failed Iraq adventure, the PNAC gang regrouped in May-2009 as 'The Foreign Policy Initiative' **(foreignpolicyi.org) to pursue the same war-based policies.**

6. American Independence and Sovereignty

The U.S. has become entangled in a host of international agreements and memberships that threaten our sovereignty, and could oblige us to go to war to protect other nations. The UN, NATO, and International Criminal Court (ICC) are old ones, but more recently we have joined GATT, NAFTA, CAFTA, and WTO. A looming (and largely secret) threat is the North American Union (NAU) idea, which some say would essentially merge Mexico and Canada with us (can you say oil?). It involves building a highway from Mexico to Canada. We should withdraw from any deal or orgs that infringe upon the freedom or independence of the USA.

A major threat is the anti-American "Law of the Sea" Treaty (LOST), or UNCLOS, was deferred again in July-2012 due to lack of votes, but the supporters keep trying. The LOST convention's purpose is to benefit Third World countries by fining and punishing the wealth and technological advantages of the industrialized West. The convention would subject our governmental, military and business operations to mandatory dispute resolution.

Any disputes would be decided by the U.N. International Tribunal for the Law of the Sea, a 21-member body representing 155 countries envious of American ingenuity and prosperity. The United States would have only one vote with which to protect American investment, and the transfer of sensitive, militarily useful and proprietary private technologies, and forced compliance with the Kyoto Protocol.

The LOST convention would be an open invitation to activist judges to interpret the convention's intentionally vague provisions against our national security and economic interests. In point of fact, were our Senate to approve the LOST convention, the odds are roughly 155 to 1 that the LOST tribunal would vote to cede U.S. claims to the North Pole and its oil riches to the Russians.
U.S. adherence to this treaty would entail history's biggest and most unwarranted voluntary transfer of wealth AND surrender of sovereignty.

The 'Cyber Intelligence Sharing and Protection Act' (CISPA), is a bill that would allow companies to bypass all existing privacy laws to spy on communications and pass sensitive user data to the government. This exposes Internet traffic, and could become an 'international' law.

7. Restitution and Compensation: 'The law

of restitution is the law of gains-based recovery. It is to be contrasted with the law of compensation, which is the law of loss-based recovery. When a **court** orders restitution it orders the defendant to give up his gains to the claimant. When a court orders compensation it orders the defendant to compensate the claimant for his or her loss.' These are both litigation situations (en.wikipedia.org)' When the government is the claimant and collects a fine from a lawbreaker, the money is usually kept by the government (another money grab!). I suggest that whenever feasible (the victims are living and known), the victims of the crime should receive the money as restitution or compensation, shared in proportion to the damage they suffered.

8. Health Care

We must end the 'Patient Protection and Affordable Care Act' (PPACA), often shortened to the 'Affordable Care Act' (ACA) and nicknamed Obamacare, is a United States **federal statute** enacted by the **111th United States Congress** and signed into law by **President Barack Obama** on March 23, 2010. Under the act, hospitals and primary physicians would transform their practices financially, technologically, and clinically in the hope of driving better health outcomes, lower costs, and improved methods of distribution and accessibility.

The Affordable Care Act was designed to increase **health insurance** quality and affordability, lower the **uninsured rate** by expanding insurance coverage and reduce the costs of healthcare. It introduced mechanisms including mandates, **subsidies** and **insurance exchanges**. The law requires insurers to **accept all applicants**, covers a specific list of conditions and **charges the same rates** regardless of **pre-existing conditions** or sex.

 Liberals/Progressives/Socialists strive for 'free' government-provided health care as a right. (Dave; Of course, any health care program is unconstitutional, except for the phony 'it's a tax' ruling by the Supreme Court), but that means nothing to most Congresspersons and voters. 'Universal Health Care' is another attempt to get 'the rich', or at least 'someone else', to pay for everything they want. I have lived in Canada and experienced the fact that when doctor's training, and then salaries, are paid by the government, 1. There are fewer doctors per 1,000 citizens, 2. Importation of cheaper foreign-trained doctors increases, and 3. The patient becomes 'more work' rather than a client they want to nurture and keep, and the level of care, caring, and courtesy declines accordingly. Most Canadians value their English roots and view the government akin to 'Mother', thus are patient with her faults, and proud (sometimes with vanity) of their traditions and Royal Family. Many view 'Americans' as relative ruffians, and self-centered , predators who don't care for each other. Hence their pride in, and patience with, their health system.

Of course, government budgets are a huge issue as to which and how much services and medicines are available, and to whom (rationing). The medical specialists and equipment for expensive services such as organ transplants are limited, and people wait for years (and sometimes die) waiting. It's the same kind of rationed care you'll find in nations like France and the England, where waiting lists for lifesaving procedures are sometimes years-long, and the death rates from breast and prostate cancer are twice to three times higher than in the United States. You can't see a specialist (ear, eye, skin, etc.) without referral by a family doctor. Old people are sometimes deemed 'not worth it' for expensive treatments and drugs.
It has been illegal in Canada to open a private 'for fee' clinic, since that is deemed unfair to those who can't afford it, but that is changing. Canadian health managers now admit that their system is financially 'unsustainable' (same in France and others), and that formerly illegal 'private services' (non-government doctors who charge a fee) and private insurance will be needed to avoid collapse. Some provinces already allow certain private services, and even pay private hospitals to take care of 'public' patients. At the extreme (Russia, etc.), corruption sets in, and doctors and staff demand bribes for access to services.

In the face of all of the above, Liberals keep pushing for 'universal health care', and they have a friend in Obama. His plan will take effect in 2014, and is expected to cost billions to taxpayers, with 'the rich' and employers targeted for most of the cost. This source of funding is a ripoff.
The cost of routine care has skyrocketed since Medicare and Medicaid were started. Health-care spending has increased from 5% to 16% of gross domestic product (GDP). Cost of these programs was the major reason, but part of the price increase is due to; 1. Loss of US Dollar value, 2. The 1986 'Emergency Medical Treatment and Labor Act' (EMTALA)

rules that hospitals must give the poor free 'exam and stabilization' service in their Emergency Centers (under the extortive threat of losing their Medicare business), and these unpaid bills are added to those who do pay, 3. Excess payments for malpractice lawsuits (reform of our tort laws is needed), and 4. Collusive price-fixing (minimum rates) set by the state-level American Medical Association (AMA) chapters and their member doctors. Further, the AMA prohibits members from advertising their rates (or skills, and track record of results). If a doctor violates the AMA rules, he/she loses their license to practice, or is harassed out of business (no referrals, etc.)! The federal government would normally attack this practice under anti-trust laws for 'collusion in restraint of trade', but the AMA has political influence, and gets a pass, which we all pay for! Also, as technology and medicines improve, people are living longer, so there are more years of illness and expenses, which often require high cost intensive care and thus higher expenses for each illness. Even young and middle-aged people may incur high expenses if costly new technology and medicines are needed. Un-funded federal mandates for free emergency service at hospitals (the Feds demand compliance or threaten to drop the hospital as an 'authorized' Medicare provider; this is an extortionist violation of rights) is often abused by illegal immigrants, or those that choose to not have insurance, and this causes higher per-day rates (to make up for non-payers) for those persons and insurance firms that do pay their bills.

Our Position: I suggest a twelve-part plan aimed at getting the government OUT of patient-doctor-hospital control and funding so that positive free-market incentives guide the patients and doctors:

1) Phase-out Medicare and Medicaid as the lower costs of free-market care become available (as described below, and vouchers in item 12), and start with having higher co-pays on Medicare and Medicaid to give incentive to avoid unhealthy life styles and non-essential visits to, and treatments and tests by, the doctor,

2) Reduce costs by greater use of Physician Assistants (PAs) so a doctor's time is not wasted on routine work the assistant can perform (including clinics run by PAs; see Item 9 below),

3) Use the FDA only to determine and disclose possible side-effects and viability of drugs, but not restrict use of them (or their potency) until there are virtually no side-effects: Let doctor judgment and CONSUMER CHOICE rule!,

4) Bring the lower price and higher quality benefits of competition, and consumer choice into health care by busting the medical pricing cartel and allowing doctors to advertise their rates (web sites ads, etc.), training and results records (see Items 2 and 9; the American Medical Assoc.- AMA- prevents this; same as ABA for lawyers) and practice as members of private, non-government sanctioned groups, rather than just the monopoly AMA; OK there are a few Osteopaths too) and state licensing boards, with all required to disclose their training and record of results,

5) Eliminate dependency on insurance provided by employers. This is a holdover from WW2 when labor was scarce, wages were limited by law, and employers used benefits to attract workers. There is no reason employers should be expected, much less required by law, to provide health insurance (see item 12 below), any more than they should provide food or clothing, to employees. It is just another way to avoid raising taxes (same as free EMTALA hospital service above),

6) Reform our tort laws to reduce excess payments for malpractice lawsuits that doctors must add to their fees. Perhaps a special court system for torts is needed (similar to bankruptcy),

7) Repeal laws that, a. Force (mandate) insurance companies to offer a long list of covered issues (let people choose the combination of coverages they want), 'community rating' and 'guaranteed issue', regardless of prexisting conditions, age, etc., and b. Limit operations to a single state. Mandating benefits is like saying to someone in the market for a new car, "If you can't afford a Cadillac loaded with options, you have to walk." The huge price increases for insurance in MA and NY show the counterproductice results of mandates.

8) Make personal payments for health insurance (but not co-pays or non-insured items) fully tax deductible,

9) Make government medical licenses optional, so we can have a wide range of private practices and clinics, staffed by 'alternate medicine' folks, Physician Assistants, retired or part-time MDs, etc., to see patients for minor problems, including issuing prescriptions for medicine. Prices will drop as the AMA cartel gets some much-needed competition.

This new approach will foster more personal responsibility by citizens (less abuse of the system; less smoking and obesity, etc.), and will give us hospitals, clinics and private practice offices offering; 'Type A' (full service, lots of equipment and specialists), Type B (moderate skills and equipment), and Type C (low cost, run by PAs and volunteer MDs, etc.; they refer cases to Type A and B as needed). This will allow people to check-out their prices, skills and record and make a choice !! With price competition, and no 'mandated coverage' plans, prices will drop, and health and access for all will improve.

If you prefer a government-licensed doctor, fine, go to one and pay more. I now hear rumors that the AMA lobby is pushing to require that PAs have a Ph.D. in nursing in order to offer the above services. YUK!; More restriction to protect the incumbent 'Cadillac' system and MDs.

10) Promote creation of private plans, such as: a) Health Savings Accounts (HSAs), funded by the person/owner or employer, which would pay for routine care and insurance for major illness. Deposits would be tax-deductible, and interest on them tax free. Each person would own theirs so no loss if they change jobs or retire, and b) Fixed payment plans (a monthly fee, no government subsidies) run by private clinics, under their own rules, that will take care of all 'basic' illnesses. . Both approaches; a) have positive financial incentives for all parties (stingy spending, shop for rates, healthy life style, etc.), b) take the government and insurance companies out of 90% of the sessions with a doctor, and c) subscribers would buy high deductible ($10,000 to $50,000) private insurance for major illnesses.
 (Note; This is similar to the voucher system in Part 12 below, but privately financed),

11) Make all State and Federal elected officials and employees (in any agency or department) subject to the same health care choices as the citizens. No special plans for health or pensions!!, and

12) To the extent that government stays involved in health care, it should; a) Be run and funded by each State, with zero Federal control and funding, b) The programs should not pay doctors and control prices, but should, c) Issue quarterly vouchers (useable only for health expenses and insurance) to 'well' citizens and permanent residents (same amount to all), but not to illegal aliens, and let them shop for the privately provided services they need, including both direct payment for routine care and insurance for major illnesses, and d) To help people caught in transition from the old system, issue special vouchers to those with major 'existing conditions' that preclude their purchasing insurance, with payments continuing until the end of their illness, or death. The value of the vouchers would be owned by each person, and could be transferred; a) to their account in another State if they move,
b) As a gift, or by a will upon death, to other qualified people, in any State. Having the programs funded and controlled at the State level has two benefits: a) It cannot be funded by fake money created out of thin air by the Federal Reserve, thus forcing fiscal sanity on the tax-funded program, and b) Having control distributed over fifty states reduces the size of the administrative bureaucracy each citizen must deal with, and makes States compete as to soundness (including sustainable funding) of their program.

To the extent that employers stay involved they can fund a 'health savings account' that the employee would own and spend (similar to a voucher). History at firms such as Whole Foods shows that employees are stingy with their account (save for future needs) and tend to care for themselves better (more diet, exercise, etc., and less smoking, alcohol, drugs, etc.) to avoid medical expenses.

Private charity (including free services by doctors and hospitals; like the old days!) will take care of the poor. This will work because with taxes and fees reduced by the above reforms there will be: a. More donations to charities, and b. Fewer people (about a 90% reduction) who can't afford health care.

In conclusion, note that none of the above suggestions depend on government rules or control of medical fees or practices. It is an ethical plan because all funding is voluntary and does not use mandatory fees, forced purchases of insurance, or coercive taxing (gang-theft-by-vote). Thus it is a fair, responsible, and sustainable plan.

****

For more info on health care plans, see:

1) www.pacificresearch.org. Their CEO, Sally Pipes, is from Canada and knows their problems well,
2) An essay from The Independent Institute:
www.independent.org/publications/tir/article.asp?a=740
3) A collection of articles from The Cato Institute:
www.healthcare.cato.org
4) 'A Four-Step Health-Care Solution' written by Hans-Hermann Hoppe in 1993
(**http://mises.org/freemarket_detail.aspx?control=279**)
5) A list of essays on health at Downsize DC, a think tank for 'less government':
http://www.downsizedc.org/bySubject/health
6) An analysis of state health programs;
'The Lesson of State Health-Care Reforms' on Oct. 6, 2009 by Peter Suderman of www.Reason.com . **Go to** http://online.wsj.com/article/SB10001424052748703298004574455560453947646

7) Senator Rand Paul, MD (U.S. Sen., KY) has proposed the "Obamacare Replacement Act" (S. 222) which is designed to 'get the gov't rules and money out of health care'. It would...

*a, Provide a two-year buffer period in which people with **pre-existing conditions (PEC)** could still get coverage **(by Redick-This is WELFARE, not insurance)**. That would allow time for the market to solve the PEC problem in other ways (as described below).

*b, Make the cost of individual insurance tax deductible. This would give individual policies the same tax treatment as employer-provided policies. Most likely, the number of individually owned policies would expand. **With more people owning their own policy,** the PEC problem would plummet. PEC is a politician-created problem that happens when people get sick after losing their job (and therefore their insurance).

*c, Give citizens an annual tax credit of up to $5,000 for contributions to an HSA (**Health Savings Account)**

*d, Eliminate the ceiling on HSA contributions

*e, Remove the stipulation that you must have a high-deductible health care plan in order to have an HSA

*f, Allow citizens to use HSA funds for insurance premiums

*g, Expand the number of things HSA funds could be used for, including over-the-counter drugs, vitamins and supplements, plus nutrition and exercise programs. One of the great flaws of Obamacare is that it does nothing to lower the burden on the medical system by preserving health and preventing disease. Healthier people don't need as much medical care.

*h, Allow citizens to band together to lower the cost of buying insurance. Individual Health Pools (IHPs) would give persons the same bargaining power that employer insurance groups currently have. The IHPs could include churches, alumni associations, trade associations, civic groups, or entities formed strictly for establishing an IHP, as long as there is no health status requirement for membership. This provision would dramatically reduce the PEC problem.

*I, Allow physicians to band together to gain bargaining power with insurers, without having to concentrate into big impersonal medical firms.

*j, Allow doctors to deduct the expense of the uncompensated care they provide, thereby making pro bono services, free clinics, and true charity hospitals more plentiful.

*k, Allow insurance providers to sell policies nationally. This would remove the cartel control that the insurance industry currently maintains through state legislatures. This would also restore the market for major medical plans, which is how insurance is supposed to work. The result would be a wider variety of policy choices at much lower prices.

*I, Give states flexibility in how they design and manage their Medicaid programs. This would enable experimentation and competition between the 50 states. It would also allow the states to innovate new ways to address the PEC problem.

*m, Repeal Obamacare at the same time it replaces it.

8) DownsizeDC.org adds; Rand Paul's plan is an excellent start. It would...

A,* Provide a two-year buffer period in which people with pre-existing conditions (PEC) could still get coverage. That would allow time for the market to solve the PEC problem in other ways (as described below).

B, * Make the cost of individual insurance tax-deductible. This would give individual policies the same tax treatment as employer-provided policies. Most likely, the number of individually owned policies would expand. With more people owning their own policy, the PEC problem would plummet. PEC is mostly a politician-created problem that happens when people get sick after losing their job (and therefore their insurance).

*c, Give citizens a tax-credit of up to $5,000 for contributions to an HSA (Health Savings Account).

*d, Eliminate the ceiling on HSA contributions.

*e, Remove the stipulation that you must have a high-deductible healthcare plan in order to have an HSA.

*f, Allow citizens to use HSA funds for insurance premiums.

---

*g, Expand the number of things HSA funds cover, including over-the-counter drugs, vitamins and supplements, plus nutrition and exercise programs. One of the great flaws of Obamacare is that it does nothing to preserve health and prevent disease. Doing so would lower the burden on the medical system. Healthier people don't need as much medical care.

*h, Allow citizens to band together to lower the cost of buying insurance. Individual Health Pools (IHPs) would give persons the same bargaining power that employer insurance groups currently have. The IHPs could include churches, alumni associations, trade associations, civic groups, or entities formed strictly for establishing an IHP so long as there is no health status requirement for membership. This provision would dramatically reduce the PEC problem.

* I, Allow physicians to band together to gain bargaining power with insurers, without having to concentrate into big impersonal medical firms.

*j, Allow doctors to deduct the expense of the uncompensated care they provide, thereby making pro bono services, free clinics, and true charity hospitals more plentiful.

*k, Allow insurance providers to sell policies nationally. This would remove the cartel control that the insurance industry currently maintains through state legislatures. This would also restore the market for major medical plans. Not only are major medical plans the way insurance is supposed to work, they are also a way to make insurance more affordable and attractive to young, healthy people. This is important because it's mostly the young who lack coverage. Obamacare used force to require young people to buy expensive plans. But Rand Paul's plan will attract them by offering them a good deal, without using force.

*I, Give states flexibility in how they design and manage their Medicaid programs. This would enable experimentation and competition between the 50 states. It would also allow the states to innovate new ways to address the PEC problem.

In short, I think Rand Paul's bill should become the official Republican bill. Regards, Perry Willis & Jim Babka, Downsize DC ,15Mar17

xxxxxxxxxxxxxxxxxxx

Again, all of the plans above (while some are better) are unconstitutional, but rely on the phony Supreme Court ruling that allows them because they are a tax. The Redick plan uses free-market competition to reduce costs and provide flexible policies.

9. Employee Unions: Unions serve a needed function when they protect members from fraud or abuse (long hours, unsafe conditions, etc.) by the employer. However, once these basic goals are met, the union managers usually try to keep or enhance their jobs (more pay and power) by seeking more concessions in the form of ever higher pay, health and pension benefits, work rules that reduce productivity, etc. As union membership declined in the 1980s, union organizers focused on government workers such as teachers, fire and policemen, prison guards, staffers, etc. (see SEIU.org and AFT.org). Refer to Stephen Greenhut's BOOK ON P. 124 'Plunder!, How Public Employee Unions are Raiding Treasuries, Controlling Our Lives and Bankrupting the Nation'.

As noted in Issue # 10 Pensions below, "In many cases, benefits became excessive when self-serving managers 'gave away the store' to avoid a strike..." Thus, there is self-serving abuse by both employer and union managers that lead to excessive costs that hurt profits and growth of the employer, or cause bankruptcy, both of which cost jobs! The US steel and auto industries are examples.

The solution is; 1) The government should not issue laws that give or allow special privileges to unions to boost their income and membership (check-off system for dues, forced union membership when hired –union shop-, guaranteed job after strike, 'prevailing wage' laws, minimum wage, etc.), but 2) Should fulfill its proper role of protecting the rights of citizens (see Issue #2, P. 41), including suits by unions due to abuse of workers by employers.

10. Employer Pensions An employer has the option of offering a pension plan to employees or not. If offered, there should be written disclosure (dated and signed hard copy) of the rules (co-payments, benefits, age and years of service to retire, restitution of equity upon termination of employment or of the plan, disclosure of fund investments, etc.), and whether the rules can be changed or the plan terminated. Just as with an insurance policy, it is the personal responsibility of the prospective employee to read and understand the plan and decide if he/she wants to work there. In recent years many plans have been changed or terminated (sometimes as part of bankruptcy) by firms in financial trouble. The government created the Pension Benefit Guaranty Corp. (PBGC) to protect workers from loss of pensions. Like most government plans it doesn't work very well. Further, it creates the perverse incentive, or 'moral hazard', of temping firms to take advantage of PBGC. The PBGC disclosed in its annual financial report that as of Sept. 30, 05 it had $56.5 billion in assets to cover $79.2 billion in pension liabilities. There has been an explosion in recent years in the number of big, ailing companies - especially in labor-heavy industries like airlines and steel - transferring their pension liabilities to the PBGC. With billions of dollars flying out of the agency's door, concern has been mounting over its financial footing. In many cases, benefits became excessive when self-serving managers 'gave away the store' to avoid a strike that would; 1) In the private sector, cause loss of profits that would hurt their next bonus, and 2) In government, cause loss of campaign donations and votes. Steve Greenhut tells the story in his book, 'Plunder! How Public Employee Unions Are Raiding Treasuries, Controlling Our Lives And Bankrupting The Nation!' (more on P. 124 and SEIU.org)

Our Position: A company need not offer a pension plan, but if it does, the rules must be published when an employee joins, and not changed without negotiation. Anything less would be fraud, and breach of contract. The governments' only role should be to require full disclosure of the rules noted above, and ongoing disclosure to confirm that the plan is properly funded. The absence of these two forms of disclosure is what has led to the painful loss of pensions by many employees.

11. Social Security

This was 20% of the FY 2011 Federal budget (started Oct-2010), thus $727 bn, and growing yearly. The present system is a welfare program for seniors, paid to them by current workers. Seniors have no equity (ownership) of the amounts they have paid-in to FICA in their working years (and contributions by their employers) and the government can stop paybacks (checks from the government) to seniors at any time. It is a devious plan and must be reformed before it fails (goes broke due to more recipients than payers) and hurts many people who are planning for it, or already dependent on it. My transition plan is to; 1) Keep the present plan in force for people age 55 or older, make paybacks proportional to amounts paid in (now immigrants get nearly full pay, with a low history of pay-ins), extend start date of payback to age 70, and grant equity ownership for pay-ins made, 2) Reduce payback amounts as needed (due to reduced program income), with five years advance notice, 3) End 'contributions' by employers, and 4) Allow people age 18 to 55 to join the new plan or go 'on their own'. Either way, they will get credit/payment for their prior pay-ins, and interest.

The current program is immoral because it depends on robbing the younger generation for 'contributions' (pay-ins) sent directly to current 'recipients' of paybacks (there is no 'fund', just bonds, –IOUs-), and is unsustainable because costs are rising while 'contributors' are declining in number and income. **The proposed new program below, 'Forward-USA Private Pension Plan'**, is similar to the plan in Chile since the hugely successful new version started in 1981.

(see; **http://www.cato.org/pubs/policy_report/pr-ja-jp.html**). This link was written by José Piñera, who as Chile's Minister of Labor privatized the state pension system, is President of the International Center for Pension Reform and co-chairman of the Cato Institute's 'Project on Social Security Privatization'; Cato.org. Our Plan is optional (individuals join if they wish) where citizen contributions would be invested by private investment fund firms chosen by the citizen, and the citizen would own the account equity. Growth in value would be tax free. A government regulatory body would set some broad investment diversification rules, to avoid high-risk or politicized investments by the fund managers. The contribution amount (weekly or monthly; a percent of pretax pay, or other personal funds) would be chosen by the citizen based on his choice of retirement age. This would encourage middle-class and low income people to start an account, which they would normally view as 'only for the rich'. This program has proven very popular in Chile (90% of workers joined!) due to the ownership aspect, which fosters personal responsibility. There are many side benefits such as increasing capital available for investment (by the pension fund firms) which reduces unemployment, plus better social and economic conditions in Chile. Go to the Cato.org link above for more details.

The 'private' and 'personal' aspects of my Plan will lead to more personal responsibility in our society, including more work, saving and good relations with the family and friends who will help care for the aged. Poverty cases can be served by private charity. The attitude of 'the government owes us everything' and 'it's OK to take others people's money to pay for my benefits' will fade. Thus, my plan is both moral and sustainable.

12. States' Rights (Federalism): The 'Articles of Confederation' were considered too weak on national defense and other matters, so a convention was called to strengthen them. This evolved to writing an entire new Constitution, which was completed in 1787. At first the States were sovereign and dominate and the new nation was referred to as '..these united States'. This soon evolved to 'The United States of America' and States' Rights kept getting weaker, especially when the federal government got control of the monetary system in 1913 with creation of the Federal Reserve System (more below). Our constitution grants enumerated powers (a list; if it's not there, you can't do it) to the Federal government (hereafter 'DC'), and by the 10th amendment, all other powers to the States, or people. Over the years, Congress, the President and courts have twisted the 'general welfare' and 'commerce' clauses of the Constitution, and invented the 'implied powers' concept, to grant enormous powers to DC, including overriding existing state laws. The Founders knew it was good to have differences between states so citizens could 'vote with their feet' if laws and taxes got oppressive. This is why U.S. Senators were to be appointed by their state legislatures, so they would better represent the interests of the states in DC (ended by the 17 th Amendment). Part of the reason the DC involvement has grown is that they control the monetary system (run by the Federal Reserve System, 'Fed') and, since leaving the gold standard in 1971, can create money out of thin air! The size of the DC piggy bank is only limited by politics in the short run, and hyperinflation and bankruptcy in the long term, and this why states become dependent on DC money for education, health, police, and many other functions normally paid by the people or state. States love getting this money, and Congressmen love taking credit for them (it's called 'pork' to get votes and campaign donations), but it comes with strings attached ('You must do X or we will stop sending money for Y'). Thus, DC feels free to impose unfunded mandates such as free emergency health care, and immigrants/refugees, on the states, and activate the National Guard (originally State Militia), without the Governor's permission. Now the Dept. of Homeland Security is sending equipment and money to local police so they can do their dirty work. The police love the new money and power!

Our position: Federal power and spending must be pushed back. The Fed's have no business in education, overriding state laws, drugs, abortion, police, and a long list of other state and local issues ! The Federal government should not be involved in an issue, unless empowered by the Constitution.

13. Privacy and Personal Liberty

A. National ID Card: Support for a national ID card (with the same info imbedded in drivers licenses) is growing and must be stopped. Abuse is inevitable in this type of federal system.

B. Wiretapping: Tell your representative to protect Fourth Amendment guarantees against warrantless searches:

Repeal the Protect America Act. The PAA legalizes warrantless wiretapping of U.S. residents, which the Bush Administration secretly began in 2001, and violates the Foreign Intelligence Surveillance Act (FISA) and the Fourth Amendment. (**H.R. 3773 and 3782** would repeal the PAA.)

Restore the requirement for individualized warrants for wiretapping of U.S. communications and email. U.S. Intelligence agencies cannot oversee themselves. The judicial branch has a necessary role in preventing abuses of power. (**H.R. 3782** would restore individualized warrants for any wiretap of U.S. calls or emails, whereas **H.R. 3773** would permit the wiretapping of some international calls and emails of Americans without individual warrants.). **No immunity for telecommunications companies that broke the law by permitting the government to conduct surveillance of their customers' phone and email records.**

To grant those companies retroactive immunity condones presidents and private industry collaborating to ransack the public trust. (Neither H.R. 3782 nor H.R. 3773 currently grants immunity, but administration allies may introduce amendments that do so.) **Let the public see the text of Congress's bills BEFORE they are passed.** Fourth Amendment rights to privacy are among our fundamental and inalienable rights. The specific text of any bill that may affect these rights must go before the American people for comment.

14. Separation of Church and State:
Persons of faith sometimes complain that their right to engage in religious activities is unfairly restricted. They say our Founders were Christians, so the USA is a Christian nation. Well, they were also white males; does that make us a white male nation? Solutions are usually sought in the 'Establishment Clause' of the First Amendment, or 'Freedom of Speech'. I say this is the wrong approach since these clauses are only about the government; 1) Not naming and supporting a certain religion (as had been done in Europe and some states), and 2) 'The free exercise' of the religion chosen by an individual. As shown in 'Our Core Principle' (item 2 above), property rights need to be superior to personal rights (such as religion) to avoid conflicts. This applies to many subjects and situations.

Our position: We recommend a property rights approach. While it is compulsory to abide by the laws of the government where you live, religion is an optional and personal choice of each individual. Laws and rights of others must not be violated in the practice of religion. Our constitution protects us from tyranny of the majority. Thus, religious groups should not attempt to mix government and religion, even when in a majority (or active minority), since it imposes (by force of law for coins, pledge), or insertion into government events and places, owned by all (schools, buildings, prayers at events) their option on others. The U.S. has complete freedom of religion so people can engage in their religion as much as they like **on their own time, events, and property.** However, just as it would be trespassing for a preacher to enter a private home or event to conduct a service, no religious group can use or adorn property, objects, procedures, or events owned in part by others (such as the government) without the permission of ALL owners (not just a majority), or their authorized agent. This applies to coins, the Pledge of Allegiance, public schools, non-church meetings, displays in government buildings, prayers at public meetings, even if attendance to such events or displays is optional.

A similar issue of trespassing would apply to Islamic mosques using loudspeakers for 'call to prayers' if they create unwanted noise in the neighborhood. The noise should be stopped on the basis of violating the neighbor's property rights ('quiet enjoyment' laws and precedents).
 Bush-43's 'faith based' subsidies to religious groups are an obvious unconstitutional ploy to promote religion, and should be stopped. Further, it harms religious work by making such groups dependent on government handouts, and subject to its rules (strings attached).

Religion obviously should not be part of our relations with other countries as to special treatment abroad, or with their lobbies in the U.S. (can you say Israel and AIPAC?).

15. Education

Today's K-12 government schools offer essentially only one flavor of education. In some districts parents can choose a school, but this offers minimal variation. They all preach 'government approved' mush that promotes government as the source of 'good and nice' things, and hide the many lies, and unconstitutional, criminal acts of the government, at all levels. Administrators have a perverse incentive to promote poorly educated kids to keep them enrolled so the state and federal money keeps coming. Our students test lower than students in European and Asian schools under similar circumstances. A big part of the difference is the poor work ethic we engender in our kids due to lack of discipline, including almost no risk of expulsion for causing trouble.

Our position: Education of children is the responsibility of parents as to amount and type. The same benefits we enjoy from a free market in food, cars, etc. (as to variety of types, and cost) would apply if schools were all private (for profit or non-). By paying tuition, parents would instantly 'be involved' to be sure they were getting their money's worth. School administrators would treat students and parents as customers who seek a good service, and can shop around for it! Good teachers would get raises the same way an engineer does (ask if you feel you deserve it, or quit and go to a competitor). They now risk loss of accrued pension benefits, but this would not apply under my plan in item 10 above. Good teachers attract customers. Parents would monitor curriculum content and teacher quality and negotiate for changes, or leave. Poor quality schools would be exposed by independent testing services or college entrance exams. This would reduce incentive for administrators to engage in grade inflation, because they would get caught.

We suggest, 1) Allow creation of private non-profit schools without government license or controls (except fraud, a proper government issue), 2) Phase-out property taxes as a source of revenue for government schools (payments have no relationship to having kids in school), and replace with tuition, 3) Terminate the federal 'No Child Left Behind' program as too costly, mostly counterproductive, and an unconstitutional violation of states rights, 4) Eliminate the federal Dept. of Education, and 5) Write tax laws that encourage donors to create scholarships and endowments to provide affordable access to these private nonprofit schools for needy students. All these changes will allow parents to choose the school that best fits their children's needs (including religion) instead of pouring more tax dollars into the present failing system. 'Do-gooders' will complain that the above approach does not guarantee a certain level (to 9th or 12th grade?) for every child due to negligent or poor parents. They prefer equal mediocrity for all. However, history shows that incentive, parents, and liberty produce much better results than government schools, while private charity helps those in need.

16. Environment

It is important to not cause excess pollution, erosion, floods, noise, odors, or other changes to the natural state that creates hazards or violate property rights, or threats thereto. Remember, your property not only includes land, buildings, cars, etc., but also your body, thus health hazards are included.

Our position: Most problems can be handled from a property rights perspective by suing the source for restitution (not just a fine paid to the government). For example, toxic smoke, underground or surface liquid toxics that enter your body, land or other property can be litigated as property damage. Nuisance items such as odors and noise that come upon your property are the same. For non-owned items such as wild animals, protective legislation can be passed, but it is important to not violate other property and personal rights (such as farmers) in the process.

17. Immigration, and Border Security

Problems: Having a 'Work Permit' (green card), becoming a 'permanent resident' or citizen of the US is a privilege that should include a set of rules and obligations. You must apply, be accepted, and follow the rules, or don't come. Our country was built by immigrants who came here to work, be free, adopt the USA as their new homeland, and become Americans (use our language and laws), and that is still desirable. But now, in addition to jobs and freedom, free health, education and other benefits are part of the attraction, and most immigrants (legal and illegal) have no intention of assimilating as Americans. Many citizens, legislators, and foreign governments, want to use immigration as a 'social refuge system' which allows the poor and displaced of other nations to come here and be taken care of (welfare, etc.), rather than work to cure the problems in their homeland. Thus, the Federal government deposits hundreds of Somalis, Hmong, Russian Jews, etc. in communities, without permission of the State government or community. More federal unfunded mandates, arrogance and loss of States' Rights! **Thus the US has become a 'salad bowl' instead of a 'melting pot' and many immigrants become a burden on our benefits system.** They often replace citizens working in low-paying jobs, adding to welfare costs and cultural stress, especially for blacks. Many unskilled citizens have lost their jobs to illegal immigrants. The 'illegal aliens' (a term often replaced by 'undocumented', as if they are victims or otherwise legal) are a further risk because they bypass checks on health and criminal records.

Illegal aliens take advantage of our freedoms by getting bolder and publicly demanding 'immigrant rights' (in-state tuition to college, health/welfare benefits, free K-12 school, etc.) even though they are trespassers in our land. The Mar-2006 mass demonstrations in many US cities are a good example. They were timed to occur a week before Congress started debate on new laws.

Minimum wage laws are a big part of this problem. Most laws require pay of $7 per hour or more, and many jobs don't justify this pay (i.e., employer can't make a profit), so employers look for other solutions. Cheap immigration labor is one alternative because they will work for cash at under $7 hour (this saves FICA payment for the employer also). It is said that Americans won't take the below minimum wage jobs, so immigrants are needed in order to get unskilled work done. WRONG! Americans will do the work, but **minimum wage laws prevent them being offered** at low rates. If the competitive market doesn't support the prices needed to cover the high minimum wage, the jobs disappear, or are secretly given to illegals. **When displaced by cheap illegal immigrant workers, our unskilled citizens may just go on welfare, leading to cultural problems and higher government expenses. Illegal immigration is not the answer to achieving price reductions!** Most politicians ignore illegal immigration because: 1) cheap labor is sought by their campaign donors, or 2) immigrants are likely to vote for politicians who hand out the free services (in most states it is easy to just get the ID needed to register from a trash bin). Illegal immigration is increasing because of: 1) the ease of walking over the border, 2) the corruption and restrictions that inhibit creation of jobs in their homeland, and 3) lax enforcement by the INS at the border and in the US.

The government of Mexico lobbies against US immigration reform because it wants the $20 billion dollars per year their people in the US send home (known as 'remittances'). After oil, this repatriated money is the second biggest source of income for Mexico.

The Mexican government also encourages illegal immigration because it relieves pressure to reform the government socialism and corruption that reduces job creation in Mexico. Their Ambassador refuses to use the term 'illegal' in reference to those who sneak over the border when interviewed on TV, and they published a booklet to assist illegal entry.

Few people know that Mexico has many restrictions on Americans who live there. Americans cannot own property, or get citizen-style health and education benefits, such as they demand here. **While the Mexican government not only requests, but claims special rights for 'their people' in the U.S., it is a FELONY to be an illegal immigrant in Mexico, subject to fines, imprisonment and deportation. What dishonesty and chutzpa !! What a bizarre one-way deal they are demanding!!**

Our proud and historic tradition as a 'melting pot' is being abused. There are lumps and islands in the pot made of people who are here illegally, or refuse to assimilate.

Our Position: 1) Employers should be required to verify legal status of all current employees and then all new hires, of any ethnic group (hence, there would be no charges of profiling), and have the government ship the illegal persons home. Once the word is out that deporting is being done, many would leave on their own.
2) Border restrictions, and temporary resident permits, should be enforced. Laws against harboring criminals and abetting illegal acts should be enforced. This will stop the work of bleeding-heart liberals and misguided religious folks from encouraging and performing illegal acts.
3) The 14 th Amendment should be revised or interpreted, so 'birthright citizenship' does not apply to children of illegal aliens. Since the loosened rules in the Immigration Act of 1965 a flood of immigrants, then their relatives, have come to the US primarily for jobs, and benefits, and most have no intention of learning English or assimilating (i.e., becoming 'Americans').
4) Proficiency in English should be a requirement for citizenship. The U.S. should adopt English as an official language for all government documents and discussions, including voting info. This will reduce costs, and encourage assimilation. Having public documents (by both business and government) issued in multiple languages, and so-called

'multiculturalism', creates a trend toward cultural disintegration in any country. The 2006 riots in France, Germany, Australia, and England are examples of the results.

5) Immigrants must agree to follow U.S. laws. If you want to live under Islamic 'Sharia', don't come! Religious activity, such as Islamic calls to prayer on loudspeakers which cover a neighborhood, must be treated as a violation of the neighbor's property rights.

6) The concept of 'hyphenated Americans' (such as 'Mexican-, and African-American') should be discouraged (but not made illegal), since it tends to slow assimilation and create separate sub-cultures. This hyphenation is a sign of resistance to assimilation (a desire to keep your group separate). There should be an oath (spoken, written, witnessed, and signed) upon becoming a citizen that the person will adopt the USA as their new homeland, and give it their first loyalty above their religion and former homeland.

7) Enforce the fact that illegal immigrants have no 'rights' except humane treatment while they are being deported!

In March-2006 there were huge demonstrations in many U.S. cities by immigrants (legal and illegal) demanding there self-made 'rights' that they claim are about the same as U.S. citizens!

One of the best solutions is to improve the legal immigration process. Excessive delays (years), and rude staff (both are typical problems in government programs), cause many otherwise honest immigrants to sneak in.

18. Private Property and Eminent Domain

Private property rights are the foundation of a just and prosperous nation. History, and the world today, shows that justice and prosperity are reduced by lack of such rights. 'Partial Takings' abound due to down-zoning of property by the government at all levels (Federal to city). An example is when they rule that, to maintain 'open space', a farmer can't lease a patch of his ground along a road to a billboard firm.

At the very least, he should be compensated for loss of income, and land value. The examples are legion. **If the 'community' wants open-space, let them pay for it!** The same logic applies for abuse of eminent domain, where 'public use' is applied to taking (owner is forced to sell at an appraised price) someone's home so a business that sells to the 'public' can use the land for a store, condos, etc. Liberals like to take money from 'the rich' using 'gang theft by vote' to fund their projects, so it is only a small step to use eminent domain to take land! We must stop this abuse.

19. Gun Ownership

Activist groups have attempted to limit private gun ownership by citing the threat of accidents in the home and killings (single or mass) by crazed or criminal people. They attempt to eliminate damage by deviates and criminals by restricting everyone. The Dec-2012 Newtown, CT killings prompted Pres. Obama and other to seek prohibition, and other restrictions, on a long list of guns.

Our Position: The second amendment to the Constitution is usually cited as the legal basis to own a gun, but this is related to state militias (why else mention it). In fact, gun ownership is an inherent right, the same as owning a potentially lethal device such as a car, knife or ball bat, and **it is only improper use that should be subject to public concern or government regulation**. Concern over gun abuse is more emotional than real. The record shows that most gun-owners are very safety conscious. Since the 1930s the population has more than doubled, the number of guns in the US has quintupled, yet firearm accidents have been cut in half. A 2002 study in Maryland shows firearms average 0.8% of unintentional deaths in over the 18-year span. As to hazards to children in the home and family life, drownings take more lives of children under 14 than firearms by a factor of 18 over the period. Even knives, bees, and scissors take more children's lives than firearms. More children suffocate (e.g., choke on solid food) by a factor of 16 than die from firearms. Here are some key causes of gun abuse:

1. As to killings by criminals, the government's war on drugs has created drug dealer turf wars that account for over 90% of deaths by guns in the U.S. These killers can get guns no matter what restrictions are put on purchases!

2. In some cases in the last ten years, the crazed killer may have been affected by medicines that control depression, anxiety, etc., as discussed in this link http://lewrockwell.com/rappoport/rappoport13.1.html .

3. Video games and movies often show violence and killing as part of the fun kids have.

4. Another stimulant may be to copy the immoral and illegal 'justified' killings that our government does when they invade nations for political (control) and economic (oil) reasons. Killing becomes viewed as 'normal' and 'routine'. 5. There is a high correlation between culture and gun abuse. Chicago and DC have some of the toughest gun laws, but are on top of the abuse list. A high population of black people applies to both (and Detroit, Baltimore, New Orleans, etc.). See this link by W. Williams Ph.D. (a black man); http://lewrockwell.com/williams-w/w-williams156.html

All the above issues and facts are ignored by the gun grabbers! In England, Canada, and Australia where gun ownership is highly restricted, burglaries and muggings (even daylight home robberies) have increased because criminals feel safe. The deterrent effect that your target person may have a gun is gone. In states where concealed-carry is allowed, muggings and armed-robberies decrease because criminals are afraid their targets may be armed. The same applies to schools where the principal or a guard may be armed. I say activists should focus on real causes and leave responsible gun owners alone.

20. Social Programs; Welfare and Culture

Our vast social programs, preferred minorities, and uncontrolled immigration, are destroying our culture. We are at the 'tipping point' in many areas where benefit recipients and new (often illegal) immigrants control the vote. Government has become Mother and Boss, and people become dependent and demand handouts and other special treatment as 'rights', rather than working for their own success. Ethics are in decline because one's reputation matters less when a person is shielded by Mother's laws. Law breaking and misconduct thrive.

We want all levels of government to 'back off' and let people manage their own affairs and interaction. Private welfare and counseling (such as Red Cross, Salvation Army, Goodwill, churches, private orgs, etc.) will serve the truly needy well. Further, private groups require less than half as much money to do the job due to better efficiency, and reduced overhead, fraud and abuse. The end of the 'entitlement' attitude and laws will cause people to manage their lives better. There will be fewer self-made 'victims' ('underpriviledged', 'disadvantaged'), and more 'responsible citizens'.

Humans thrive in an environment where they are comfortable with the region's personal value system, laws, religious attitudes, etc. This gives the feeling of 'home'. A common language has a lot to do with this bonding.

Today, a high percentage of immigrants (legal and illegal) have no intention of assimilating. They are only here for jobs and benefits. This will lead to strife for all.

History and logic show that my 'less government intervention' approach not only yields more liberty, but more peace, justice, prosperity and better ethics. This approach **rewards personal responsibility and work,** and private charity cares well for the needy (withh reduced perverse incentives-i.e., 'career' welfare users-, and lower costs due to use of volunteers, and no 'entitlements').

The 'more government' systems, **such as pushed by Progressives, Liberals, and Socialists, have the opposite effect**, and do more harm than good (counting side-effects)

When people become dependent on government, they care less about support from, and relationships with, friends and family. **As these relationships whither, other social problems such as crime, broken homes, and laziness grow.**

21. Gay, Ethnic, and Hate Laws

There are many conflicts in the law as to what gays (homosexual persons) can do. Marriage and adoption are active now. Most churches view gay conduct as a sin (i.e., wrong even if you are not violating or threatening another's rights; see issue 2, 'Core Principle' above). Of course, those who consider it a sin (or on any subject; abortion, gambling, etc.) are free to peacefully promote their views, short of violating the rights of the so-called 'sinners', by setting an example with their conduct.

I view these conflicts as examples of why the government should abolish laws that control our lives by favors and restrictions (i.e., social engineering). Marriage is a personal matter **and none of the government's business** (it started with laws to prevent –white-black marriages!). Favorable tax laws for married persons should be abolished. A 'marriage contract' will handle inheritance, etc., and should be used by all; gay and straight. Adoption should be controlled by the birth parents and private orgs.

Laws giving any group special rights and preferential treatment (which creates a 'preferred minority') should be abolished also. Such laws are easily abused by ethnic persons or groups. For example; 1. In Oct-2007, the former football coach of a major U.S. university won a $2 million judgment claiming the school fired him because of his race (black), not his 6-27 won-loss record, and 2. A minority person now feels free to park illegally (including at the front door!) of a shopping center, or post office, etc., since usually no one will challenge them for fear of a lawsuit, or being attacked! 'Hate Crime' laws are another example. There should be no 'special' penalties; murder is murder. **All citizens should have the same rights, with no special rights or privileges for gays, or any other group, as to race, sex, economic or social status, religion, etc. (see 'Core Principle' in Issue # 2 above).** People should be able to associate with (or avoid) whomever they want without fear of lawsuit for violation of special 'civil rights' privileges, and the same applies to clubs, employers, etc. as to membership, hiring, and firing (short of violating a person's legal rights). This approach leads to a just and harmonious society, where people learn to 'get along' without government coercion.

Restrictions and favors do more harm than good as to improving social, and economic success of minority groups. Special rights and subsidies reduce incentive for self-improvement, and create the opportunity to abuse such rights. Intrusion in people's lives is unconstitutional and none of the government's business.

22. The Drug War

Our legal system for drugs is antiquated and distorted with hypocrisy and inconsistencies. 'Drugs' such as nicotine and caffeine (stimulants, uppers) and alcohol (a depressant, downer) are legal to use and available anywhere. They are both damaging to health, but are legal for political reasons (voter demand, campaign contributions), and because the government wants the tax revenue. Other uppers and downers are illegal. Extracts of marijuana with proven medicinal uses are illegal, while morphine (made from otherwise illegal opium) is used by doctors for pain suppression. Why is one OK and not the other? Changes are needed. While excess use of 'sporting' drugs is a serious medical and social problem, only fools and ignorant youths do it. However, I say criminalization of such stupid activity only makes it worse (our experience with alcohol prohibition is a good comparison). Further, such use is none of the government's business unless the user violates or threatens someone else's rights (see Forward-USA 'Core Principle' in issue # 2 above). The FDA and our 'War on Drugs' do much more harm than good. Users can get drugs easily even after years of the Drug War (but they cost more now), and the violent 'turf wars' of pushers and gangs (and now murder of law enforcement people by cartel thugs; TX first, Chicago next?), plus burglaries and muggings by users to support their habit, are worse than ever. **It also corrupts police**; 1) With the easy abuse of 'asset forfeiture' laws. They can be imposed as 'civil' arrests on just 'suspects'; no profit on illegal acts; they can confiscate – and own – any asset that was 'associated' with a 'suspected' crime. This includes local police taking title to, and selling (their department keeps the money!), cars, boats, planes, ranches, etc. without trial. The owner can sue for return, but this takes time and money and may not work, 2) By hiring military vets (trained to kill, not protect) to get more free military equipment, and 3) By the funding and excitement from SWAT Team 'combat' style attitudes and raiding equipment.

Our solution is to treat drugs like alcohol and nicotine (tax it and control age of buyer and offer optional control on purity of product), and handle abusers as; a) A mental and medical problem, or b) Illegal if a user threatens others, such as driving a car while high. Abuse and violence will soon subside, just as with alcohol, after the end of prohibition. The fact that many drugs are more potent than alcohol makes it even more urgent to get such business out of the hands of criminals.

23. Energy Problem: Energy costs and consumption are going up worldwide, while oil reserves and production (barrels per day, B/D) from exising wells are going down. The world's daily production averaged 83 million B/D in 2004, and the USA consumed about 25% of it (with only 4% of the world's population). Production of 'cheap oil' (cheap to find, pump and refine) is forecast to decline to 39 mill. B/D by 2030 while consumption increases to 118 ! This is the 'peak oil' concept, where wells in liquid oil pools start to produce less per day. The difference will have to be made up by coal, natural gas, tar-sands, shale-oil and gas (by 'fracking'), nuclear, wind, solar, and bio-fuel, algae farms, etc., plus reduced consumption and more CONSERVATION !! Each fuel has its own economic, technical, and enviro issues. Oil has been cheap to get, and convenient to use, so has been the first choice so far. As the price of oil goes up, these alternate fuels will become more attractive, especially if renewable and/or sustainable. Consumption by China and India is growing faster than any other country. They are shopping for long-term OIL DEALS, big time! This ties-in with why Bush invaded Afghanistan and Iraq, and Obama is threatening Iran (as I write in March-2013); namely to control the Greater Mid East oil producers (including Uzbekistan, other 'xxstans', the Caspian area, and North Africa) before other countries make deals for it. An underlying reason is to prevent access by China, thus limiting their growth. USA leaders want it ALL! Our Position: **We recommend; 1. End the Afghanistan and Iraq wars, and engage in peaceful oil-supply negotiations with all producers worldwide (we are a big customer, and they need us!), 2. Allow eco-friendly oil drilling in all parts of the USA. Note that the Audubon Society has done this in their preserves, 3. Encourage development of alternate fuels and methods (such as electricity from new-generation engines, solar, hydro and nuclear, but no subsidies; end the counterproductive corn ethanol**

program), and 4. Allow gas and oil prices to rise to their free-market levels, without subsidies or control, but with appropriate anti-pollution laws based on property-rights (protect your body, water, air, and land) for those people and places at present or future risk. The past errors, distortions and fears of nuclear energy need to be updated and corrected so the new and safe methods for generation of electricity can be employed. Safer thorium could replace uranium.

24. Traits of Capitalism and Corporations; Liberals, Socialists, and Progressives like to attack 'Capitalism' and label it as a 'social system', and 'corporations' as bastions of greed and abuse. However, Capitalism is properly defined in my 1953 and 1961 dictionaries as an 'economic system' based on private ownership and free enterprise. It is also a moral system because all conduct is voluntary. Current dictionaries have crept toward defining it as a 'social system' as Liberal editors take control; very convenient, but false. A Corporation is just a legal structure to allow shared ownership and financing. Liberals like to say that corps are a way to avoid personal responsibility! These definitions were invented by Liberals as straw men to avoid their own complicity in corrupt and unconstitutional government. It is bad 'people' (as usual; same for churches and governments), bad laws, corrupt government (including legal 'favors', subsidies, etc.), and perverse incentives that cause the trouble. Liberals avoid criticizing government because they want it to keep giving the legal favors and welfare, but only to their projects. What a pile of ignorance and hypocrisy! For example, the June 26, 2002 main editorial in the Wall Street Journal, by Dr. Henry Manne (George Mason Univ., Univ. of Chicago, etc.), made a great point that the Williams Act of 1968 (now rules 13d and 14d of the 1934 Securities Act) was the birth of the Boardroom and Officer fraud and self-dealing we have been seeing since the '80s (it took a few years to set in). The new
law required takeover groups to announce their intent once

---

they had 5 % of the target stock, which gave warning so officers could protect themselves. This allowed officers of many firms to get lazy and corrupt without risk of getting booted-out. Remember, corporations become takeover targets only because their profits, and return on assets, are low, usually due to bad management. In takeovers, the shareholders win, but bad managers lose! Thus, at-risk bad managers whine to the government for protection (can you say 'campaign donation'?). Many states have passed laws to 'protect' their local firms from 'outsiders', and the 'poison pill' was born to fend-off the takeover groups! Another factor is the shareholder laziness that developed in the 1990s as stock prices soared due to inflation. The attitude was 'all's well', 'no worries'. It wasn't long (and quite predictable) that the nomination of Directors by shareholders was restricted, and biased 'Buddy' Directors were selected by Officers (a 'slate'). The self-dealing started, and the combined 'Chairman and CEO' position was born (an inherent conflict) ! These hot-shot CEOs plundered their firms with huge salaries and stock options, while trying to set a glorious, resume-enhancing, growth record with short-term, unsustainable, profit enhancements (reduce staff, announce grand plans, etc.), and excess debt, spending and risk They often got themselves and their firms in business or legal trouble, but left with 'golden handshakes' or hung around a while with 'retention bonuses'. There are hundreds of examples! Why should a low-performing, or corrupt, CEO get a multi-million dollar bonus when fired?? It is white-collar theft! The Dodd-Frank bill of July-2010 issued a vast set of rules to correct abuses, but puts a major compliance burden on firms.

Solution: We say the solution is to repeal the Williams Act, and other distortions of the free market, not pass a slew of new regulations. Let the free market do its work, so shareholders will wake-up then nominate and vote for honest, competent Directors that select and monitor the officers.

25. Origins of 2008 Crash and Effect of Bailouts

The rush of home loan defaults and bank problems started in late 2007, and peaked in Sep-2008, and is continuing, but less, at this writing in Nov-2016. The underlying cause was Fake Money, as described in Chapter 3. This excess supply of money, delivered to lenders by the Fed and its pals at FreddieMac and FannieMae, was the 'mother's milk' of market distortion. A trigger was the 4.25% increase (from 1% to 5,25%) in interest set by Greenspan when he ended his Fed term in Jan-2006.

A major facilitator was the Community Reinvestment Act (CRA), a 1977 federal law that requires **banks** and **thrifts** to offer **credit** throughout their entire market area and prohibits them from targeting only wealthier neighborhoods with their services, a practice known as "**redlining**." The purpose of the CRA is to provide (force?) credit, including home ownership opportunities, to 'underserved' (unqualified?) populations and commercial loans to small businesses. OK, getting their votes may be part of it!

The CRA was passed into law by the U.S. Congress in 1977 as a result of national **grassroots** pressure for affordable housing, and despite considerable opposition from the mainstream banking community. The CRA mandates that each banking institution be evaluated to determine if it has met the credit needs of its entire community. In 1995, as a result of interest from President Clinton's administration, the implementing regulations for the CRA were strengthened by focusing the financial regulators' attention on institutions' performance in helping to meet community credit needs. These changes were very controversial and as a result, the regulators agreed to revisit the rule after it had been fully implemented for five years. Thus in 2002, the regulators opened up the regulation for review and potential revision.

The **Clinton** Administration's regulatory revisions with an effective starting date of **January 31**, **1995** were credited with substantially increasing the number and aggregate amount of loans to small businesses and to low- and moderate-income borrowers for home loans. Part of the increase in home loans was due to increased efficiency and the genesis of lenders, like **Countrywide** (set up as an 'off brand' by Bank of America), that was aggressive and did not mitigate loan risk with savings deposits (ie, borrowers must have deposits) as did traditional banks using the new subprime authorization. This is known as the secondary market for mortgage loans (high risk for banks). The revisions allowed the **securitization** (packaging, with insurance, and called AAA; FRAUD!!) of CRA loans containing **subprime mortgages**. The first public **securitization** of CRA loans started in 1997 by **Bear Stearns**, and it helped break them in Sep-2008! The number of CRA mortgage loans increased by 39 percent between 1993 and 1998, while other loans increased by only 17 percent (a flood of money into high risk).

In the 1980s, groups such as the activists at ACORN ('Association of Community Organizations for Reform Now', **www.acorn.org**; an Obama favorite!) began pushing charges of "redlining" - claims that banks discriminated against minorities in mortgage lending. In 1989, sympathetic members of Congress got the Home Mortgage Disclosure Act amended to force banks to collect racial data on mortgage applicants; this allowed various studies to be ginned up that seemed to validate the original accusation.

In fact, minority mortgage applications *were* rejected more frequently than other applications - but the overwhelming reason wasn't racial discrimination, but simply that minorities tend to have weaker finances. A study in 1992 proved that bias was not the problem. Yet the harm was done and banks loosened their rules to avoid lawsuits.

A good example is an article on the government's takeover of Chrysler as written by Peter Schiff (see P. 127) on May 5, 2009 and quoted in part here: *"...A real bankruptcy is the only solution. In it, current shareholders get wiped out, current contracts and obligations are voided, which creates the opportunity for new management, with private capital, to scrap out-of-date business practices, and produce cars cheaply and profitably. Under the guise of 'saving jobs', the Administration has disrupted this process."*

Illegally giving control of Chrysler and GM to the UAW and the government in 2009 enshrined a culture of failure and sealed Detroit's fate. Both companies have become government-sponsored entities, not too dissimilar from Amtrak or the Post Office, forever relying on taxpayer funds to create products of dubious quality." Sure enough, Detroit is now full of decay and crime. The police have given-up on serving some neighborhoods!

The statist approach of Obama's 'government intervention and control' will make the economic recovery worse and longer. His re-election in Nov-2012 adds to the potential amount of economic and cultural damage!

26. Occupational and Business Licenses:
Problem: Licenses are touted as a way to protect citizens from faulty or fraudulent services, but in fact usually limit choices to the citizens and give 'cartel or monopoly' status to the license holders. This applies to lawyers, doctors, plumbers, beauticians, restaurants, contractors, etc. where the licensing is often abused by; 1. The government, and incumbent licensees, to restrict new entrants in order to protect themselves and friends from competition, and 2. By associations (unions, medical, legal, etc.) to impose rules such as minimum fees to clients, controlled or no advertising of rates, etc. The government has threatened cancellation of a license to force 'cooperation', such as making phone companies give them private usage data, or radio and TV treat

them 'nice'. Another category is when the citizen is subject to, or can be threatened by, the service provider without initiating choice. An example is a truck driver or airline pilot, where one can be run into, or be in a crash, if an unqualified person is providing the service. These should be licensed to PROTECT the citizen, a proper function of government.

Our Position: We recommend that licenses be **optional** when the citizen can initiate choice of the service provider (you can't on an airline, etc.). This would; 1. Allow individuals and firms to offer services, and set and advertise prices, without permission from the government or a 'professional society' or union (let the buyer beware, and decide), 2. Allow groups to form 'professional societies' or unions that set their own standards of quality, disclosure of member skills and performance records, and membership requirements, and advertise them, without government control, and 3. Bring the benefits of competition (better quality, lower prices) to the trade groups (yes, doctors and lawyers are a trade group). Buyers who prefer a government-licensed provider, could use one; but all buyers (patients, clients, etc.) would have a CHOICE of licensed or unlicensed. Of course, it follows that the chooser would be responsible for the results and could not sue a vendor for being incompetent if unlicensed.

27. Limits on Terms and Benefits for Congress

Problem: One cause of corruption in DC is that officials will do almost anything to keep their prestigious and profitable jobs (pork to voters; favors to campaign donors, etc.). Furthermore, they vote themselves pension, health and other benefits that far exceed what they bestow on their constituents.

Examples are; a) Better pensions and health care than Social Security and Medicare, b) Their children can include student loan debt in a bankruptcy, c) Any campaign funds existing when they retire can be used by them for non-personal spending (but they often benefit). Can you say 'Privileged Upper Class'?

Solution: We recommend that: 1. No U.S. Representative may serve more than four terms (8 years), two terms (12 years) for a Senator, or a combined fourteen years if they have worked in both jobs (based on a combined life total), 2. All elected officials get the same pension (Social Security) and health (Medicare) benefits as the 'common' citizens, and with the same rules for calculating fees, and reimbursement of claims, and 3. End any other special treatment that is found.

28. Eliminate 'Earmark' Pork Funding

Problem: Most Congresspersons like to 'bring home the pork' to fund state projects and win votes. These 'earmarks' are hidden, unconstitutional, add-ons to other funding bills such as transportation, and 'Omnibus Appropriations Bills' (5 or 10 funding bills combined), and are not discussed in the normal approval process, yet add-up to billions of dollars per year. Even worse, the omnibus bills are usually many hundreds of pages and few Congresspersons read any part of them! Since the government is already 'in the red', this spending is a serious add-on to our national debt problem!

Solution: We should promote a bill to make earmarks and Omnibus Appropriation Bills (and sneaky 'Minibus' bills) illegal for all Congresspersons. This will eliminate cries by some voters of; 'We're not getting our share of pork'. Of course we will also fight for reductions and elimination of improper grants and subsidies. Unfortunately, in May-2009, Pres. Obama blessed earmarks by saying; 'The local Congressperson knows best what his/her District needs.' Another campaign pledge trashed!

29. Nullification of Federal Laws by States: In general, nullification is refusal to enforce a law deemed unconstitutional or otherwise illegal. It originates in the concern of government becoming too strong or abusive, and ignoring the Constitution and laws. Key applications are;

1) Refusal of States to enforce Federal laws; **State sovereignty over the Federal government is the basis. Recent examples are** state nullifications of all, or portions of, the REAL ID Act of 2005, medical marijuana laws, Cap and Trade, and the Second Amendment restrictions

2) Refusal of a jury to enforce charges imposed by a law or the court; This **relates to sovereignty of the citizens over all levels of government. On this basis, juries can refuse to impose the penalties decided upon by the court. Over the years, judges and lawyers have made nullification illegal, confirming the original concern; They want more power!**

Our position is that nullification is necessary as a check on excess and immoral use of power by the government. Tom Woods Ph.D. explains it well in his book; 'NULLIFICATION: HOW TO RESIST FEDERAL TYRANNY IN THE 21ST CENTURY' ON P. 1XX.

30. Secession by States from the USA: The USA was created by secession of the colonies from England. The new 'states' were sovereign entities that created a Federal government, limited in scope by a Constitution. It was voluntary, thus any member could leave

Early examples of 'creeping federal dominance' that violate our freedoms and States' Rights were: 1) The Civil War (actually a war of aggression by the North; the South just wanted to leave, not take-over the government) established the Federal government as superior in power to the States based on 'might-is-right', and 2) The Pledge of Allegiance, written in 1892 by Francis Bellamy (a socialist Baptist minister who was fired for his socialist sermons) which included the word 'indivisible'. In 1954, Congress after a campaign by the catholic Knights of Columbus, added the words, 'under God', making the Pledge both a patriotic oath and a public prayer. Both terms are improper because; a) our allegiance should be to the nation (the land and people), not the government, and b) 'under God' violates separation of church and state (inserting religion into a text, place, etc. that is used, and owned, by all).

Recent Federal mandates (Obama's health care, 'No Child Left Behind', TSA, drug laws, etc., etc.) have awakened interest in secession because they violate the Constitution, States' Rights, and our fundamental rights of self-government, and voluntary association. Groups in many States have sent secession petitions to the White House! Secession is a proper reaction to abusive and illegal acts by the federal government. As a first step, secession petitions can be a tool to alert Congress and the President to the need for changes. Opponents cite the Article 6 'Supremacy Clause' in the Constitution (which can be argued only applies to laws that are Constitutional). The Swiss use their Referendum process to change laws and terminate the jobs of politicians. We should do the same. In the absence of corrections from DC, full secession can be employed (similar to referendum in #31 below; also see   # 12 States' Rights).

31. Constitutional Amendments:

a. Referendum Laws : The Swiss have a system of 26 cantons which have comprised the federal state since 1848. The citizens have been very successful in controlling government abuses and excesses by use of their referendum laws which allow them to; 1) Remove legislators from office (recall), 2) Pass laws that they want but can't get the self-serving legislators to pass, and 3) Repeal laws that they don't like. This keeps the legislators alert to comply with the voter's wishes, and gives voters incentive to be active (awake) in managing their country (rather than whining as 'victims'). In the U.S., 'States' Rights' would be strengthened by this approach (see #12, p. 73 above). See Ron Holland's plan on p.105. My plan (p.103) suggests a similar set of rules be invoked, and

b. A Balanced Budget amendment will give us a powerful tool to limit spending. Politicians will like it because they can claim; 'We want to give you more, but our hands are tied!'

32. Abortion

Problem: There will always be abortions. The legality and conditions are what vary. Roe v Wade, and government payments in many cases, have made abortion so cheap and convenient it is often treated as a means of contraception. Carelessness and irresponsibility are rampant.

Our Solution: I am personally opposed to abortion except to protect the mother's life, and say in no case should the government pay the costs. I further oppose abortion after the first trimester (3 months is plenty of time to make up your mind), and all partial-birth abortions. However, one should not seek laws to force others to comply with one's own value system. Again, the 'Core Principle' applies (see Item 1b above). The question is. 'When does the fetus become a separate person with rights?' Many people take the position that abortion is a moral or religious issue, and assert that 'life begins upon conception' and the fetus is an 'unborn child', This is a sincere position, but we must not negate the fact that **the fetus is not a separate person with rights until detached from the Mother (umbilical cord cut).** Until then, it is a living part of the mother's body, like her arm and heart, but not a 'person' with rights.

As to the law, a woman's body is her property, and does not belong to the government, her doctor, or her church. Thus, it is a woman's right to make an informed choice on what happens to her body. **In fact, for a responsible woman there are a series of three choices involved.** Whether to;
1) Have sex,
2) Use protection, and
3) If pregnant, deliver a baby, or have an abortion.

The Roe vs Wade ruling is invalid because the Federal government has no constitutional authority in this area. Thus it is a State issue. In summary:

1. Opponents of abortion should not attempt to impose their personal views or religious beliefs on others by force of law. That would be **immoral and unconstitutional**. They should peacefully oppose abortion without using force or threat to the pregnant woman, or her doctors and staff and their facilities.
2. Proponents should exercise their right without expecting others (including via the government) to pay for it, and they should observe the three choices above.

33. End of Life Choices: Modern technology allows terminally ill people to live longer, but usually at great expense and suffering (a socially mandated form of torture). To avoid this harm, our laws and societal standards need to be revised as follows. Current law gives four choices for the patient and family; 1. Increasing pain medication (for comfort), 2. Terminal sedation (keep the patient completely unconscious until death occurs), 3. Withdrawing treatments and life-support (no water or food), and 4. Advance authorization to doctors and family filed by the patient while healthy as a 'living will' and/or 'power of attorney'. Self-inflicted, and patient-approved 'assisted suicide' are illegal (remember Dr. Kervorkian?), but this ignores that in a free society you own your life and body (the government and church don't). It is none of the government's business what you do to yourself, thus should be legal. 'Mercy killing' (no patient approval), is illegal due to possible misuse, but should be made legal with adequate controls (such as family approval when available; always a medical statement that the subjects' comatose is incurable). Moral and religious issues are optional personal choices. Note that the above changes do not grant any legal authority to the government. It is all about personal Liberty.

Blank

Blank (**reserved**)

Chapter 5: Rebuild America

The following 'Rebuild America' plan to create a better future of liberty, peace, justice, and prosperity for all.'

As you read this chapter, please keep in mind this fundamental issue: Our Founders wrote in the preamble, **'We the People ... do ordain and establish this Constitution...'.** I say the time has come for We the People to re-ordain and re-establish our Constitution, and **make** our government officials, and judges, comply with it by engaging in a non-violent rebellion. Most (well over 50%) of our laws and spending since 1932 and ALL of our wars since 1776 have been unconstitutional, and started based on lies (see Appendix 1; P.131, 'Wars and the Lies that Start Them'). The result has been a serious cultural (more irresponsible and illegal conduct, violence, and corruption by citizens and government) and economic (excessive spending, taxes, and debt) decline in the USA!

It is time to fight back to restore the rule of law, and stop the abuse and crimes done by self-serving politicians and their corporate and 'more-government, Progressive' friends!

The list of issues in Chapter 4 must be dealt with. Please do your part by choosing a topic there and working to solve it. Owners of this book are authorized to copy pages and send them to their federal or state legislators to urge them to act on my recommendations.

An important goal of the plan is to restore traditional Republican principles, and compliance with the Constitution.

We should focus on the federal government in DC because it does the most harm with unconstitutional wars, fake money, plus excessive spending, taxes, and debt. This is only possible with fake money that is also the world's primary 'reserve currency', since people, firms, and banks, at home and worldwide, will accept it for payment and keep it as a safe 'store of value'. Thus, only the USA can pay its bills with an unending supply of new money. This feeds the spending, excessive imports (thus 'off shoring of jobs), welfare, pork, wars, and corruption in the USA! It allows DC to impose unconstitutional 'national' laws (on abortion, drugs, free emergency care at hospitals, etc.) that pre-empt state laws and prerogatives, because the State's executives are shameless beggars and must comply or lose some funding. This free ride will end when the world tires of accepting our fake money due to fears our economy is failing. This tragic end of our fake prosperity started with the massive Keynesian-style 'Quantitative Easing' (QE-1, 2, 3-infinity; flood the economy with money!) 'stimulus' programs by the Federal Reserve, started in 2009 and funded by newly created fake money which will eventually result in major price inflation (caused by a major loss of US Dollar value; 50% or more?)!! This approach ignores the need for Supply-Side-style 'investment incentive' tax reductions and low regulation to revive the economy and create new jobs (P. 146). The USA is now likely to decline (by 2016, 2020?) to a middle-class 'post-empire' nation, operating on a smaller budget. The examples are former 'empire nations' such as England, Spain, and France. Refer to Chapter 2 'Empires'. David Stockman gives a tough description of our problems in his new book 'Deformation' (P. 152)

One benefit of the USA being 'cash-creation-limited' will be the termination of wars, foreign bases, and foreign 'aid' (bribery) we can no longer afford; A classic case of doing the right thing for the wrong reason.

A major economic development is occurring in the U.S. due to development of 'fracturing' methods for releasing gas and oil contained in shale rock deep underground. The estimated reserves, and building the wells to tap them, could make the USA the leading producer and exporter of oil and gas in the world! This would be a 'game changer' that could; 1) Increase Federal revenue from various fees, and thus reduce our debt, 2) Create jobs, and 3) Help Pres. Obama 'squeeze by' the 'fiscal cliff ' his spending has created! His post-election approval of the final portion of the Keystone pipeline to deliver tar-sands oil from Canada to refineries in Houston will add to the revenue. We'll see!

Ron Holland offers a plan in his series 'How to Restore the West' (with '12 Axioms'), which propose state sovereignty, and more, as a way to avoid collapse of the USA. See this series at; www.thedailybell.com/28523/Ron-Holland-How-To-Restore-the-West, and more about Holland at P. 124. Another approach (insurance instead of gov't) is offered by H. Hoppe at **http://lewrockwell.com/hoppe/hoppe32.1.html** . See Don Miller's '14 Point Plan' on p. 149.

The above plans are compatible with mine below, but I offer more details. You can see a copy of this entire book at Part 1 in the left margin of my Forward-USA.org site. Some of the topics in the plan have been discussed in prior chapters, but the Plan ties them together.

A Plan to 'Rebuild America' by Restoring Government to Its Proper Role'

The USA is at a tipping point where spending and tax reductions and legal reforms must be made or we will have a more severe economic crash than we have experienced since 2008. Due primarily to increases of our money supply (monetary inflation) to support government spending, the US Dollar (USD) has lost over 95% of its purchasing power since 1913 (when the Fed started), and faces further losses if we don't reduce spending soon. The GOP 'Path to Prosperity' plan by Rep, (and former VP Candidate) Paul Ryan sounded good, but only asked for minor spending cuts while saying nothing about our failing monetary system and costly military bases and wars (only military 'inefficiencies'!). His Mar-2013 plan showed a debt payoff by 2023, but with $2.3 tn more tax revenue! The world views us as a failing empire and other major nations are making preparations to replace our dominance in financial and political matters, including the USD's status as the world's primary 'reserve currency' (any seller or lender will accept and keep it), which allows us to create new money to pay our bills! (and we abuse it!). In 1968, then French President Charles de Gaulle called it our 'exorbitant privilege'. The plan in Chapter 5 to 'Rebuild America'' shows how we can reduce our arrogant excesses and avoid an economic and political crash.

The Original USA Attitude

Let's look at our nation's history to see how we got into the economic and cultural mess we are in.

The USA has evolved in government and geography in many steps. When the thirteen colonies in America won their independence from England upon signing the 'The Paris Peace Treaty of 1783' on September 3, 1783, they were referred to as '...free sovereign and independent states..' In order to better coordinate their activities and defense, they created the 'Articles of Confederation' on November 15, 1777, then the 'US Constitution' on September 17, 1787, and the USA was born! Both of these documents; 1. Treated the States as sovereign entities, and 2. Were a specific list of limited powers and duties granted to the central government by the States and people. The concept was (and is) that if the power to do or legislate something is not granted therein, the government has no authority to do it, except by amendment.

The settlers came to America seeking freedom and took great care to not grant too much power to their new government. It was viewed as a servant created to only protect the rights of its citizens from violation by others, not to 'manage' the economy or people. Key words are 'protect rights', and 'by others'. Under this legal system you can do whatever you want if you don't violate the equal rights of others (of course 'non-legal' social issues such as honesty, courtesy, etc. still apply). The rights are limited to one's natural rights (such as free speech, property rights, freedom to travel and associate, etc.) that are free and you are born with. They do not include; 1. So called 'legislated rights' (or 'entitlements'), all unconstitutional, that have been created by improper government, and 2. Goals and desires such as health-care, education, housing, jobs, etc. A guide is that 'nothing can be a right if you expect someone else to pay for even part of it'. Sounds good for the start of a new country, but it hasn't worked out as planned!

Personal responsibility was emphasized in early America. Families and private charity, with voluntary donations, took care of the needy. But over time, politicians seeking votes have created 'benefits', 'subsidies', and other favors for people, businesses, and activist groups that have created dependence on the government and have become viewed as 'normal', and 'the American Way' (entitlements). FDR launched the 'paternalistic' style government in 1933 as his solution to the Great Depression, which was caused by excess money from the Fed (see below). Private charity has waned as the government became the source of funding (easier than seeking voluntary contributions).

Since 1782, the governments at all levels (city, county, state, federal) have expanded their role to become a manager, and then controller, of the people and economy, with vast powers to restrict liberty and force compliance to the dictates of politicians, who in turn are often controlled by other groups (corps, unions, activist groups, etc.). The result is that we now have an overbearing government that creates war, debt, and restricts liberty. Police, the TSA and other law enforcement groups often act as aggressors and bosses, rather than helpers to protect the people. The federal politicians, with their lust for power and endless source of fiat paper are the worst violators and cause damage both at home and worldwide.

How the USA Government Grew and the People's Attitude Changed

First, let's look at the major events that enlarged and molded today's USA:

1. 1861, the Civil War; **Postured the federal government as superior to the states.**

2. Wars of aggression to add land and colonies; 1812-'War of 1812', Attempted to acquire Canada; 1839-'Mexican American War', Invaded and acquired the northern half of Mexico, now most of the SW 6 states; 1898-'The Spanish American War', invaded and acquired Puerto Rico and Guam, bases in the Philippines, then 'annexed' Hawaii. For details on our wars of aggression, see Appendix 1, P. 131. Lands acquired by negotiation were; 1803- Rights to French 'Louisiana', 1822-Florida Territory, and 1846-'Washington Territory' by a treaty.

3. 1913, Federal Reserve System; **The Fed; created by and for politicians and bankers to provide a near endless supply of money and credit to serve them.**

4. 1917, US entered WW1 and **became a world power, and the US Dollar a reserve currency** (held by banks as reserves, and used for international transactions)

5. 1933, President F. D. Roosevelt (FDR) launched the Social Security System, the FDIC, ended private ownership of gold, and started many other social and economic programs; **The birth of 'paternalism'.**

6. 1941, US entered WW2 (to assure Germany didn't win and become a world power, instead of the U.S.), and by 1945 became the world's top power, with the US Dollar the world's 'official' (based on Bretton Woods decree, not usage) reserve currency (redeemable in gold at $35 ounce, but only between nations); the start of **world domination and Empire-USA.**

7. 1965, President L. B. Johnson **launched Medicare (A & B), and Medicaid**. Now 'others' will help pay your bills!

8. 1971, President Nixon ended connection of the USD to gold. Money creation and prices have soared since then; **The start of extreme excessive spending and debt** by the people and government.

The above events created a huge Federal government with worldwide 'interests', all unconstitutional. Now more people work for various levels of government (22.5 mill.) than in all manufacturing (11.5 mill.). This is about the opposite ratio of 1960. (To be fair, the productivity of the average American factory worker has tripled since 1972, so total manufacturing output should not be measured by the number of people employed) **Most people now view government as 'mother' and 'manager'. This creates dependency, careless living, and reduces initiative and personal responsibility**. Immoral gang-theft-by-vote (targeting any person or group that has money) is accepted by most as a normal way to raise money, and is a sign of cultural decay. Our nation has become 'Empire-USA'. Politicians now see the world as their domain, and the 'military-industrial complex' pushes (and bribes Congress) for more foreign wars and occupations to feed their business'. The massive problem we now face is that all empires in history have failed due to; 1. The expense of constant remote wars for control and resources (now oil, etc.), and 2. The decline of productivity at home, and demands for benefits (food, housing, health, pensions), by the people. This is the USA we see around us today; A failing empire! For more on empires, see Chapter 2, and Appendix 1, P.131.

A Plan to Restore Government to Its Proper Role

This plan shows how to restore control to the people, abolish unconstitutional spending, conduct, and laws (including the Federal Reserve System and undeclared wars), cut taxes, and end abuse of the 'interstate commerce' and 'general welfare' clauses in the Constitution, thus allowing USA citizens to enjoy more liberty, peace, prosperity, morality (more honesty and courtesy; less force, theft and fraud), and justice. All changes shown below should be made as soon as possible (1 to 5 years max.), depending on the size and complexity of the issues.

All financial experts agree that a country is in big trouble when its debt exceeds its GDP. See Table 2 on P. 48 for our dangerous debt problem. "Progressives' (people who seek more government spending and control to solve social and economic problems) complain that 'cuts' to their projects are cruel, but ignore the greater pain caused by the economic crash that their unsustainable spending and government intervention in the economy has caused. The economic problems since 2008 are just a start. When speaking to these Progressive groups as a candidate, I have asked if anyone supports 'gang-theft', and none say they do. Yet they all support immoral gang-theft if done by voting to target and tax anyone with money such as 'the rich', 'inheritors', or 'corporations', even if gained honestly and with taxes already paid. This is very convenient compared to soliciting voluntary contributions, but very immoral and counterproductive, and one of the signs of decadence in a failing empire. Of course the business groups (the 'Military-Industrial Complex') and politicians that support invasions, wars, and occupations for economic and political gain (Iraq, Afghan, Libya, etc. for oil and control) for Empire-USA are an equal or bigger part of the moral and economic problem we have.

The legal limit on our national debt has been increased by Congress in twelve steps from $5.5 tn in April, 1996, to $10.62 tn in July, 2008 (grew $5.1 tn in twelve years; $425 bn average per year). We exceeded the legal debt limit of $14.29 tn set in February, 2010 (grew $3.67 tn in 2.5 years; $1.5 tn average per year, triple the rate of the prior twelve years!!). Due to the Wall Street bailouts in 2008, and the Fed's program of 'Quantitative Easing' (pouring new money into the economy), **the annual rate of debt growth has increased faster in the last few years, and is expected to grow even faster in the years ahead!!**

The 'cuts' now planned in Congress do not come even close to avoiding a crash of our economy and the US Dollar. I credit Sen. Rand Paul for his ongoing efforts to; 1) audit the Fed, 2) fight the terms (loss of civil liberties, etc.), and excessive funding of the NDAA bill, and 3) filibuster against using drones to kill citizens in the U.S.!

Details of the Rebuild Plan We Propose:

My transition plan is to; 1) Keep the present plan in force for people age 55 or older, make paybacks proportional to amounts paid in (now immigrants get nearly full pay, with a low history of pay-ins), extend start date of payback to age 70, and grant equity ownership for pay-ins already made, 2) Reduce payback amounts as needed (due to reduced program income), with five years advance notice, 3) End 'contributions' by employers, and 4) Require people age 18 to 55 to join the new plan or go 'on their own'. Either way, they will get credit/payment for their prior pay-ins, with interest.

1. **Monetary System:** (This is a summary of a large topic. For more detail get my 'Monetary Revolution USA' book at Amazon.com, or see the text at part 2 in the left margin of my site Forward-USA.org).

We now have what is known as a 'fiat' monetary system, where the value of paper money (Fed notes) and coins is the 'face value' declared by the government, and must be accepted for payment because of 'legal tender' laws. The paper notes are not redeemable in a commodity with market value such as gold, and the coins are made of cheap 'base' metals such as copper, zinc, nickel and steel (not even a portion of 'precious' metals such as gold or silver). This system allows the government to create paper and 'digital' money 'out of thin air' and funds the wars and corruption we now have (without the politically sensitive use of tax increases). The redeemability of Fed notes for gold by other nations was ended in 1971 by Pres. Nixon (because we were running out of gold), and creation of new money has soared since then. As a result, the USD has lost 82% of its value (purchasing power) since 1971, and 98% since the Fed started in 1913 !

We have abused our money by excessive creation of new dollars, and other nations (who own 32% of our debt) now fear their holdings of dollars will lose most of their. China and Japan are the most exposed (with about $1.2 tn each of US debt), with S. Korea next, all due to acquisition of dollars from their exports to us. Other nations, led by the BRICS (Brazil, Russia, India, China, and South Africa; Japan too, more soon), are holding formal meetings to consider alternatives to the dollar. China is ending many restrictions on use of its yuan currency, and increasing its gold reserves, so it can be used in world trade and investments. The US may opt for a new currency via the IMF to pre-empt collapse of the USD, and claim (lie) that the new money (Bancor, or SDR?) is a big improvement. The IMF decreed the Yuan will be added to the SDR basket in Oct-2016. This is expected to have a major impact on value of the USD, and its' status as the primary worlds' reserve currency. Precious metals could rise.

We must end excessive expansion of our money supply. **This is what has funded our excessive imports that result in 'offshoring' of jobs and factories'!** My proposed Forward-USA solution is to immediately abolish the Fed and legal tender laws, allow free-banking (no license or location limits, just full disclosure of assets and liabilities), allow private mints, make all current Fed Notes redeemable in gold by anyone on demand (and create no new notes, physical or digital), and use gold in coins (such as a small disc in the center). This is the classic 'Gold Standard'. It prevents the government from creating money 'out of thin air', ends the moral hazard (doing risky deals because you expect to be bailed-out if they fail) of 'lender of last resort' to banks, makes bailouts 'unfundable', and has always resulted in more prosperity and fewer and smaller wars and business cycles. There will be no 'run' to get rid of Fed Notes because they will ALL be redeemable in gold the day the new system is announced (100% reserves in my plan). The amount of gold per current Fed Note dollars would be set by dividing the amount of gold we own (8,134 metric tonnes; subject to audit) by the number of dollars issued (M3, about $14 tn), which yields two ten-thousands of a troy ounce per dollar, or $50,000 per ounce with current 'dollars'. After the new system starts, Fed notes would be exchanged for new money denominate in weight of gold. Prices (and government taxes and fees) would also be shown in weight of gold (such as one-half ounce, or 15.6 grams, for a car). Once the US converts to gold, all nations will, or Sellers won't accept their trash fiat paper; Good! Governments hate the restrictions imposed by the gold standard (limited supply) so fight the ascendance of gold as shown in Dr. Robert's article 'Assault on Gold'; P. 126.

Of course, it follows that we should resign from the meddling groups such as the International Monetary Fund (IMF), World Bank, Bank of International Settlements (BIS), and the G-20, all of which only exist to patch and pamper the world's fake money system. For more detail, refer to essays in Appendix 2, P.159.

2. Spending, Debt, and Taxes

Summary: In fiscal year 2011 (ended Sep. 30, 2012) the federal budget was $3.708 tn (24% of GDP, and is expected to grow to over 30%, UGH!), and they expect to spend $1.65 tn more than they take in (the annual deficit). Our $16.3 tn total national debt (as of Nov-2012), and the interest on it, are growing rapidly. Debt held by the public (mortgages, credit cards, etc.) is about $13.9 tn. Unfunded debt for future entitlement costs is over $181 tn!! (Table 2)

> **a) Taxes** (all levels of government; city, county, federal): As explained by 'Supply-Side' economic policy (see P.C. Robert's book on P. 126), low taxes and regulation, are the first steps to renewing investor confidence and creating incentive for producers to expand their firms. This leads to new jobs and economic recovery. Our complex tax laws are often immoral, and always costly to comply with and enforce. Many taxes and deductions are part of the government's social and economic planning (which they shouldn't be involved in at all), and often do more harm than good. Again, Liberals-**Progressives reject the incentive logic of how lower taxes create jobs**, and prefer to increase taxes on 'the rich' to make them pay their 'fair share'. They purposely ignore that the top 10 percent of income earners pay about 70 percent of all federal income taxes though they earn only 43 percent of all income. Isn't that enough??

Solution: I recommend; 1) End the capital gains, personal income taxes, and phase-out property taxes (use tuition for schools; see P. 77, #15), 2). Start a Federal sales tax (around 15% would probably work; adjust as reduced spending occurs) with no deductions (not a VAT with hidden layers), 3) Charge 'User Fees' wherever practical. This would apply to now free services such as libraries, pools, and highways (more than now), and 4) Convert our monetary system to the gold standard (see P. 33, 111).

b) General Domestic Spending: This is now 32% of the Federal budget. The changes I suggest below will save about $500 bn per year (50% of current budget). We should; 1. Eliminate unconstitutional cabinet-level departments (Education, Energy, Agriculture, Homeland Security, HUD, 'Health, Education and Welfare', etc.) and just retain parts of Commerce, Defense, and Treasury, 2. End all programs such as National Endowment for the Arts, National Endowment for Democracy (NED; this is often used to illegally fund and organize revolutions in other countries), NPR, Peace Corps, AMTRAC, Import-Export Bank, AFDC, Food Stamps, Unemployment Pay, 3. End Pell Grants and Tuition Loans for college students and grants to professors (they flood the college industry with money and allow excessive spending and tuition increases by colleges), etc., and 4. Reduce FDA, and EPA to advisory roles, with enforcement by states. Welfare programs such as AFDC (Aid to Families with Dependent Children) actually lead to more broken families as some fathers leave when they qualify for AFDC or rent subsidies. These 'social' programs are justified as serving the 'disadvantaged' or 'underprivileged'; notice the 'victim' orientation of these terms. Conversely, Progressives view successful people with good incomes as 'privileged' or 'lucky' and say they should be forced to pay higher rates called their 'fair share', better called 'a penalty on success'! The top 10% of earners already pay about 60% of the tax dollars received by the government; isn't that enough?? Note that 'dollars paid' is what counts, not percent. All of these 'social' programs are unconstitutional, and must end. Some are desirable, but should be funded by voluntary donations (private charity). 'Privatization' of many current government functions (roads, schools, utilities, medical, pensions, transportation, etc.) is a proven way to cut costs.

c) Social Security: This was 20% of the FY 2011 Federal budget (started Oct-2010), thus $727 bn, and growing yearly. The present system is a welfare program for seniors, paid to them by payments from current workers. There is no 'Trust Fund', just a bucket of IOUs! Seniors have no equity (ownership) of the amounts they have paid-in to FICA in their working years (and contributions by their employers) and the government can stop paybacks (checks from the government) to seniors at any time. It is a devious plan and must be reformed before it fails (goes broke due to more recipients than payers) and hurts many people who are planning for it, or already dependent on it.

The current program is immoral because it depends on robbing the younger generation for 'contributions' (pay-ins) sent directly to current 'recipients' of paybacks, and is unsustainable because costs are rising while 'contributors' are declining in number and income.

My proposed new program, 'Forward-USA' Private Pension Plan', is similar to the plan in Chile since the hugely successful new version started in 1981. José Piñera, who as Chile's Minister of Labor and privatized their state pension system, is co-chairman of the Cato Institute's 'Project on Social Security Privatization'; (Cato.org). See it at; **http://www.cato.org/pubs/policy_report/pr-ja-jp.html.**

My Plan is optional (individuals join if they wish) where citizen contributions would be invested by private investment fund firms chosen by the citizen, and the citizen would own the account equity. Growth in value would be tax free. A government regulatory body would set some broad investment diversification rules, to avoid high-risk or politicized investments by the fund managers. The contribution amount (weekly or monthly; a percent of pretax pay, or other personal funds) would be chosen by the citizen based on his choice of retirement age. This would encourage middle-class and low income people to start an account, which they would normally view as 'only for the rich'. This program has proven very popular in Chile (90% of workers joined!) due to the ownership aspect, which fosters personal responsibility. There are many side benefits such as increasing capital available for investment (by the pension fund firms) which reduces unemployment, plus better social and economic conditions in Chile. Go to the link above for more details.

The 'private' and 'personal' aspects of my Plan will lead to more personal responsibility in our society, including more work, saving and good relations with the family and friends who will help care for the aged. Poverty cases can be served by private charity. The attitude of 'the government owes us everything' and 'it's OK to take others people's money to pay for my benefits' will fade. Thus, my plan is both moral and sustainable.

d) Medicare and Medicaid; This was 22% of the FY 2011 Federal budget (started Oct-2010), thus $846 bn (and growing yearly). The changes below will save about $300 bn per year (35% of current), with Medicaid funding shifted to the States. End both programs at the federal level over a five year transition period (to allow people to make changes) and replace it with my free-market plan shown in Chapter 4, item 8 on P. 63. This plan emphasizes use of Health Savings Accounts (HSA), owned by each person (and useable in any state, or as a bequest at death), and funded by state government, employers (at their option), and donations. The person uses the money to 'shop around' and pay doctors, clinic plans, or insurance firms directly. This has proven to reduce costs and increase personal responsibility, such as avoiding obesity, alcohol, and smoking. People are stingy with spending their HSA funds, so abuse and unneeded tests and drugs are reduced! Making all licenses optional brings patient choice and competition to the current pricing cartel held by the AMA (American Medical Association; they pay Congress well). We now have only 'Cadillac' level medical service. This plan will allow nurses (or Physician Assistants) to open their own clinics for lower-level problems, at about one-third the cost per visit! If you prefer to pay about $200 to see an M.D. for a sore thumb, fine, go to one. Some people say that others are too stupid to select non-MD services, but I say 'Mind your own business and let others manage theirs'. This attitude of excessive regulation and licensing (to protect and restrict us, and limit competition; see # 26 on P. 96) is a key reason how government and health costs have gotten too big and oppressive!

e) Defense and Foreign Spending (including foreign aid, the CIA, and all US military activities and bases): This is now about 19% of the FY 2011 Federal budget, thus $712 bn per year. The changes below will save about $500 bn per year (70% of current). We must; 1. End Empire-USA and our self-appointed role as the world's policeman (or Boss and Bully?), 2. End the illegal and immoral wars and occupations of Afghanistan (for access to build a pipeline to Turkmenistan, and land for bases), Iraq (for its oil, land for bases, and defense of Israel), and Libya (for oil and to expel China) in an orderly manner, not to exceed one year, 3. Offer reparations for our share of war damage and murdering of their people, 4. Close all foreign bases, and resign from the UN (embassies give adequate contact with other governments; the UN is a cesspool of politics), NATO, and other mutual-defense treaties, and 5. End all 'foreign aid', most of which should be called 'bribery of foreign leaders'. In general, mind our own business, use purchase negotiations rather than war to get oil, and end special treatment of Israel and any other nation that has political favor and power in the US Congress. In accordance with the reduced missions above, we must reduce; 1. The number of military personnel and facilities, and 2. Development and production of contractor-provided military equipment and services. Medical treatment and other benefits for military veterans (not contractors) should be continued; these troopers are the victims of our warmonger politicians.

f) Debt: Both federal and personal debt have soared in recent years. Loose money stimulates spending! Federal debt is $16.6 tn, debt held by the public (mortgages, credit cards, student loans, etc.) has jumped to $15.8 tn (about equal to GDP!!), and unfunded future debt (for entitlements) is $181.2 tn!! (see Table 2, P. 36).

In calendar year 2012, the U.S. government will spend around $220 billion in **net** interest on its debt, according to the Congressional Budget Office — a figure that is expected to spiral ever higher in coming years. The $220 bn is about 6 percent of the total federal budget and 1.4 percent of GDP. The CBO assumes that the yield on the 10-year Treasury will rise from an estimated 2.3% in 2012 to 5% by the end of the decade (2020); and the yield on the 3-month T-bill will increase from 0.1% to 3.8% during the same time. Current low interest rates are a key factor in keeping the government's interest expense burden low. If we don't reduce our deficits (less spending), the USD will lose its 'safe haven' and 'reserve currency' (allows creation of new money to pay bills) status and interest rates for borrowing will soar to unsustainable (unpayable) levels.

Of course, we must eventually pay the loan principal too! My plan for reduced spending will reduce risk for our lenders (less creation of new money, less loss of dollar value) and help prevent an increase in rates. If we don't reduce spending soon, we will have an economic crash similar to the PIIGS (Portugal, Italy, Ireland, Greece, Spain) in Europe, and no entity is big enough to bail us out!

g) Unconstitutional and Abusive Laws and Programs:
The list is too long to show here, but the key ones to end (not in order of importance) are;

1) The 'Imperial Presidency' and all of its 'Executive Orders' - past and future-, and 'Signing Statements', that start wars, and create or change laws, most of which are unconstitutional or illegal, and none authorized by Congress. Bravo to Sen. Rand Paul (R-KY) for his March 6, 2013 filibuster of the Brennan confirmation hearings for CIA Dir. to extract details from Atty. Gen. Holder about the rules for using drones to kill U.S. citizens within the USA!

2) 'Legal findings' and the Military Commissions Act of 2006 (MCA) that allow torture and detainment of suspects (terror and other) based only on just an accusation by an informant or government official,

3) The Patriot Act, CIA, and TSA,

4) The Williamson Act of 1968 that made hostile takeovers difficult and helped incompetent and corrupt corporate officers and Directors keep their jobs and abuse their shareholders (excessive pay, etc.),

5) The Exchange Stabilization Fund (ESF), created by FDR to distort the precious metals market,

6) The 'Real ID Act'

7) All minimum wage laws

8) All laws related to the grossly counterproductive War on Drugs (it creates more sellers-pushers, murders of police, and users), including Asset Forfeiture. It has supporters in Big-Pharma, DEA, local police SWAT teams, prison unions and private prisons, who see the War as a source of revenue and job security. A key issue is: What a person does to himself is none of the government's business.

9) The Fannie Mae (FNM) and Freddie Mac (FRE) GSEs that, with the help of Banksters and Wall Street, fostered selling 'securitized' bad mortgages worldwide, which was a big part of the crash of 2008! All perpetrators should be charged with fraud, just as they did in Iceland!, and

3. 'Referendum' and 'Balanced Budget' Amendments:

a) The Swiss have been very successful in controlling government abuses and excesses by use of their referendum laws which allow then to; 1) remove legislators from office (recall), 2) pass laws that they want but can't get the self-serving legislators to pass, and 3) repeal laws that they don't like. This keeps the legislators alert to comply with the voter's wishes. I suggest a similar set of laws be invoked in the USA, and

b) A Balanced Budget amendment will give us a powerful tool to limit spending. Politicians will like it since they can claim; 'We want to give you more, but our hands are tied!'

Summary of the Plan

If started in 2017, the above ideas and solutions will reduce total annual spending enough to create a budget surplus by late 2020. This will allow us to start paying-down our debt, and end the threat of a declining monetary system (by then on the gold standard I hope), and economy. The alternate is to keep spending and destroy the U.S. Dollar and our economy! There will be hardships as government jobs and contracts are eliminated, but with advance notice, and 'furlough pay', the pain will be less. Sadly, it must be done.

Let's get started before we crash. We owe it to our children and future generations!

****** End of Plan Description ******

How 'True Republicans' Will Implement the Plan

We 'True Republicans' are politically active because we consider it to be our duty as responsible citizens of a republic. Thus we will work to implement the 'Rebuild America' plan (suggestions are welcome).

We believe our nation is best served by a government that does not intervene in our personal lives ('social' issues), or our business affairs ('economic' issues), as long as we are not violating, or threatening, the rights of others (see 'Core Principle' in Chapter 4, #2). We like the traditional principles of: 1) Complying with the Constitution, 2) The governments' only proper role is to **protect** our personal and property rights, as individuals (no 'group' rights), from threat or violation **by others**, not to manage or control our lives (thus, you can do whatever you want if you don't violate rights of others; no 'victim'), 3) Strong homeland defense, but a non-interventionist foreign policy (with no preemptive wars or occupations), 4) Enforce separation of church and state; no trespassing or rudeness to impose your religion on property or events owned or shared by others, 5) A minimal federal government and sound, with emphasis on Federalism (States' Rights), and 6) Low spending and taxation, with a balanced budget.

True Republicans need to create a new GOP because it is time for reform and rebuilding. This requires replacing the off-course leaders to repair their damage and stop them from causing more! Their GOP goals should be more liberty, peace, justice, prosperity, and morality (more honesty and courtesy; less force, theft and fraud) for all, in the USA, and the world.

Thanks for your time and interest in reading this book. Fight hard to make the above changes, but with no violence or abuse of the personal or property rights of other people.

Thanks and Good Luck, Dave

■■

(Reserved)

Part 2:
■■■

1. Recommended Authors, Books, and Sources:

Contents: A. Authors-P.147, B. Books-P. 152, C. Internet Info Sites-P.154

A. Authors

1. Pat Buchanan: In his book **'Day of Reckoning**: How Hubris, Ideology, and Greed Are Tearing America Apart", 2006, Pat says that America is facing a crisis from which it may not survive. He argues that the effects of mass immigration, ineffective foreign policy, and an overextended military, are leading the country on a path of destruction. Pat has written eleven books including; **'The Unnecessary War'**, **'A Republic Not An Empire'**, **'The Death of the West'**, and '**Suicide of a Superpower'**, 2011.

2. Douglas R. Casey: In his book **'Crisis Investing'**, 1979, Doug predicted a major depression due to government intervention. It came in 2008! He; 1) Is an independent thinker, with 'on the ground' business experience (not biased by academic rules and vanity), 2) Supports liberty, the gold standard, and limited government as the path to peace and prosperity, and 3) Writes books about investing and government; His new book **'TOTALLY INCORRECT'**, 2012, with L. James and T. Coxon, is an unabashed treatise for libertarianism and free-market capitalism; **'Crisis Investing'**, 1995; and '**The International Man'** 1979, with H. Schulz. See his articles: 1) Feb-2012 about war, oil, gov't, and gold at: **lewrockwell.com/casey/casey108**, 2) Mar-2012, 'The Ascendence of Sociopaths in US Governance' **lewrockwell.com/casey/casey112**, 3) Nov-2012 'The America That Was – Now the United (Police) State of America', **lewrockwell.com/casey/casey139, and 4) http://lewrockwell.com/casey/casey150.html . His archives are at; lewrockwell.com/casey/casey-arch, and caseyresearch.com/cdd/archives**.

3. **Thomas J. DiLorenzo Ph.D.**, **professor of economics at Loyola University Maryland, is the author of** The Real Lincoln **(Dec-2003);** How Capitalism Saved America; Lincoln Unmasked **(Nov-2007);** Hamilton's Curse; Organized Crime: The Unvarnished Truth About Government; **and most recently,** The Problem With Socialism. He is a senior fellow at the Ludwig von Mises Institute, holds a **Ph.D.** in Economics from **Virginia Tech**, and has written for the Wall Street Journal, Barron's, and many other publications.

4. **Pepe Escobar** is a Brazilian investigative journalist. He writes great articles about government treachery for **www.atimes.com**. He has focused on Central Asia and the Middle East since the late 1990s. and is the author of the books Globalistan: **How the Globalized World is Dissolving into Liquid War** (Jan-2007), **Obama Does Globalistan,** Jan-2009, and **Red Zone Blues'** Aug-2007. He invented the term 'pipelineistan' to cover the hidden political and shooting wars led by the U.S. to control the oil and gas in the Greater Mid East.

5. **Stephen Greenhut** is Vice President of Journalism at the Franklin Center for Government and Public Integrity *(FRANKLINCENTERHQ.ORG). HIS BOOKS ARE.* **'Plunder!, How Public Employee Unions are Raiding Treasuries...'** *in 2010 (SEE SEIU.ORG), AND* **"ABUSE OF POWER: HOW THE GOVERNMENT MISUSES EMINENT DOMAIN"** *IN 2004. SEE HIS ARTICLE;* **www.lewrockwell.com/greenhut/greenhut72.1** .

6. **F. A. Hayek,** Nobel Laureate. See; **'Denationalisation of Money: The Argument Refined'**, 1976, which puts forth the case to; 1) end the government monopoly on money creation, 2) let anyone create money, and 3) let the free market determine which type of money is used.

7. **Ron Holland is an international retirement consultant, public speaker, stockbroker and author of three books (including** 'Escape the Pension Trap') **and numerous articles and special reports. He is a strong proponent of investment outside U.S. markets and the dollar as protection from America's exploding national debt. More at** www.RonHolland.com, www.bfi-consulting.com, **and articles at** www.thedailybell.com . **More at P. 105.**

8. **Laffer Ph.D., Arthur:** While on the Reagan staff in the 1980s he was one of the creators of Supply-Side Economics and the Laffer Curve, which shows the tradeoff between tax rates and revenues. His books include '**End of Prosperity**', and most recently '**Return to Prosperity**'. He earned an MBA and Ph.D. in economics from Stanford University. See more at www.laffercenter.com.

9. **Eric Margolis** wrote **'American Raj'**, 2008. He is an American with French and Canadian ties. His father was in the Foreign Service and he grew up in in the Mid East. As a long-time foreign correspondent for the Toronto Star, and others, he has traveled the world and has great insight about world events. See www.ericmargolis.com

10. **Donald W. Miller, Jr., M.D.** is a cardiac surgeon and Professor of Surgery at the University of Washington in Seattle. He is a member of **Doctors for Disaster Preparedness** and writes on politics, health and medicine. For a start, see his excellent '**A Fourteen Point Plan for a Post-Wilsonian America**' at **http://www.lewrockwell.com/orig2/miller2.html**, and his archives at **www.lewrockwell.com**. His web site is **www.donaldmiller.com**, which includes his CV and bio.

11. **Gary K. North** Ph.D. (born 1942) writes on economics, history, and theology. He received a **PhD** in history from the **University of California, Riverside** in 1972, and served as research assistant for **Congressman** Ron Paul **in 1976**
His blogs are garynorth.com, and teapartyeconomist.com

12. Rep. Ron Paul M.D. (R, TX-14), wrote **'The Revolution: A Manifesto',** April 2008, and **'End the Fed'** in Sep-2009, and was a Republican candidate for President in 2008 and 2012. Dr. Paul says we have been lied to, robbed and used by our own government. Dr. Paul ended his last term as a Congressman in Jan-2013. On April 17, 2013 Dr. Paul announced creation of his **'Institute for Peace and Prosperity',** with a mission to educate and advocate for a peaceful foreign policy and the protection of civil liberties at home **(ronpaulinstitute.org). Eric Margolis (# 10 above) and Butler Shaffer (# 18 below) are on his Academic Board.** See his archives at **http://www.lewrockwell.com/paul/paul-arch.html**, and his ongoing activity at CampaignforLiberty.org, and 'unofficial' news at ronpaul.com and dailypaul.com.

13. James Quinn, is Senior Director of Strategic Planning for a major university, and author of a series of essays on world financial affairs. See: 'WHAT HAPPENED TO THE AMERICAN DREAM', Dec. 24, 2008' at **http://www.financialsense.com/editorials/quinn/2008/1224.ht ml**, and 'The Law of Unintended Consequences: 20th Century and Beyond' Jan. 5, 2009. For more, go to **http://seekingalpha.com/author/james-quinn** , www.financialsense.com/editorials/quinn/2009/0218, http://www.informationclearinghouse.info/article33527.html and his main site; **http://www.theburningplatform.com/** .

14. Paul Craig Roberts, Ph.D., is an economist and author of eight books and many articles on economics and politics; all non-PC, based on fact and logic, and seeking the truth. He; 1) Holds a Ph.D. from the **University of Virginia**, and was a post-graduate at the **University of California, Berkeley**, and **Oxford University** where he was a member of **Merton College**, 2) Worked for Rep. Jack Kemp and Pres. Reagan on the implementation of 'Supply-Side' economics (see P. 146), leading to his book **'The Supply-Side Revolution'** in 1984, 3) Is a former; a) Associate Editor of the Wall Street Journal, b) Contributing editor for National Review, and c) Assistant Secretary of the U.S. Treasury, and 4) Is the John M. Olin Fellow at the Institute for Political Economy and a Senior Research Fellow at the Hoover Institution, Stanford University. Other books (some co-authored) are; **'Capitalist Revolution in Latin America'**(1997), **'The Tyranny of Good Intentions'**(2008), **'How the Economy Was Lost'**(2010), and **'Failure of Laissez Faire Capitalism'**(2013). His internet columns have attracted a worldwide following See his site **paulcraigroberts.org** (click 'Articles' for archives; including 'Assault on Gold'), and his full story at **en.wikipedia.org/wiki/Paul_Craig_Roberts**.

15. Murray Rothbard Ph.D., A great Austrian economist, Professor, and prolific author. See '**For a New Liberty**' and archives and books at **http://www.mises.org/money.asp**

16. Salerno, Joseph, PhD; Salerno is a professor of economics at **Pace University** (NY). He is the chair of the economics graduate program, and is also a senior faculty member of the **Mises Institute**, for which he frequently lectures and writes. He serves as editor of the Institute's **Quarterly Journal of Austrian Economics**.

17. Peter Schiff is President of Euro Pacific Capital and author of 'The Little Book of Bull Moves in Bear Markets' in 2008, 'Crash Proof: How to Profit from the Coming Economic Collapse' in 2007 (then a '2.0' version in 2011) and '**The Real Crash**' in 2012. All give 'real life' ideas for economics and investing. See his business site **http://www.europac.net/**, and archives at http://www.lewrockwell.com/schiff/schiff-arch.html

18. Butler Shaffer writes on the nature and threat of government and law in our lives. He holds both B.Sc. and B.A. degrees from the University of Nebraska, and a J.D. degree from the University of

Chicago Law School. After practicing law for seven years, he is now a professor at Southwestern University School of Law in Los Angeles. His books are; 1. Violence as a Product of Imposed Order (1976), 2. In Restraint of Trade (1997, 2008), 3. Calculated Chaos (1985, 2004), 4. **Boundaries of Order** (2009), and 5. **The Wizards of Ozymandias** (2012). See **http://swlaw.edu/faculty/faculty_listing/facultybio/70115**

19. David Stockman was director of the Office of Management and Budget under President Ronald Reagan, serving from 1981 until August 1985. His 2013 book "The Great Deformation: Corruption of Capitalism in America', discusses how central bank meddling and the breakdown of sound money have bludgeoned the free market, eviscerating its capacity to generate wealth and growth. He was a Director of www.heartlandpartners.com .

20. Robert Wenzel is editor and publisher of the 'Economic Policy Journal' (EconomicPolicyJournal.com) which provides a steady supply of free-market analysis on a broad range of topics.

21. Thomas E. Woods, Jr. Ph.D. holds a bachelor's degree in history from Harvard and his master's, M. Phil., and Ph.D. in history from Columbia University. He is the author of eleven books, most recently **ROLLBACK: REPEALING BIG GOVERNMENT BEFORE THE COMING FISCAL COLLAPSE**. More at **TomWoods.com**.

B. Books

1. **'Empire of Debt'**, a 2006 book by W. Bonner and A. Wiggins. It addresses how excessive national debt and spending can drastically reduce the value of the U.S. Dollar, and cause a major depression.

2. **'The Blowback Triology'**, three books by Chalmers Johnson (Blowback-2000, Sorrows of Empire-2004, Nemesis-2007). Johnson shows how our meddling, and expensive, foreign policy does more harm than good.

3. **'The Price of Loyalty'**, 2004. by Paul O'Neill, former Sec. of Treasury. This book describes the attitudes of the Bush cabal and how they discussed plans to invade Iraq long before 9/11.

4. **'The Fall of the House of Bush'**, by Craig Unger, 2007 (also 'House of Bush, House of Saud'); A journalist, he describes; 1. The true story of how the Bush cabal schemed to control the world for religion and money, and 2. The rise and collusion of the neoconservative and christian-right influences in Republican party politics

5. **'A Nation of Sheep'**, 2007, by Andrew Napolitano, (also 'Constitutional Chaos'), is about how Americans accept abuse by the government without complaint or curiosity, as long as the 'good times roll'.

6. **'Index of Economic Freedom'**, annual since 1994, The Heritage Foundation, charts economic success vs freedom; **www.heritage.org**/research/features/index/

7. **'The Israel Lobby'**, Mar-2006, the LONDON REVIEW OF BOOKS, an essay by John Mearsheimer and Stephen Walt, Professors at the University of Chicago, followed in 2007 by their book **'Israel Lobby and U.S. Foreign Policy'.** An analysis of the scandalous illegal and covert operations of Israel's U.S. lobby 'American-Israel Public Affairs Committee' (AIPAC) and how it impacts votes in Congress and election of Congresspersons.

8. **'The True Believer'**, by Eric Hoffer, 1951, a book which shows how people join a group or mass movement (nationalist, social, political, religious, 'Global Warming', etc.) to bring a sense of security, power, righteousness, or income to themselves.

9. **'The Great Reckoning: How the world will change in the depression of the 1990s'**, 1991, by J. Davidson and Lord R. Mogg. They warn of economic collapse of the USA due to overspending and Empire-style foreign policy.

10. Older Books that Gave Warning and Good Advice

a. **'The Law'**, 1850, by F. Bastiat. With his perspective of the French Revolution, he explains the fallacies of Socialism and how it must degenerate into Communism.

b. **'War is a Racket'**, 1935, by Smedley Butler, Maj. General, US Marines. He charges that war profiteers are behind our wars and they are all crimes.

c. 'Capitalism: The Unknown Ideal', 1967, by Ayn Rand. Discusses both the productive and moral aspects of Capitalism. Comments by Alan Greenspan (before he joined the Fed banksters in DC)

d. 'Truth and Untruth', 1972, by Rep. Paul N. 'Pete' McCloskey Jr. (R, CA-11, 1967). Pete warned us about Nixon's lies concerning Vietnam, and the broader scope of dishonesty in government. Pete was my Congressman, and I helped in his first election campaign in 1967.

e. 'A Time for Truth', 1979, by William Simon. Bill warned us of the damage being caused by excessive spending, taxes, and the debasement of our currency.

f. 'An American Renaissance', 1979, by Rep. Jack Kemp. Jack sent an upbeat message on how less government spending and lower taxes would produce more growth, all based on his support of Austrian economics. His landmark **'Economic Recovery Tax Act of 1981' (Pub.L.** 97-34), also known as the **ERTA** or "**Kemp-Roth Tax Cut**," was a federal law enacted in 1981.

g. 'Restoring the American Dream', 1979, by Robert Ringer. Robert warned us of a trend in the USA to expect a 'free lunch', and how we can reverse the trend with more personal responsibility and less government.

C. Info Sources on Economics and Government:

Articles & Politics; AmericansforProsperity.org, **ActivistPost.com, LewRockwell.com, Antiwar.com, FFF.org, VDare.com, Reason.org**, Cato.org, **PacificReasearch.org**, pgpf.com, conservativehq.com , **Independent**.org, PacificLegal.org , RLC.org, Mises.org, Senateconservatives.com, Freedomworks.org

Data:
en.wikipedia.org/wiki/Money_supply, en.wikipedia.org/wiki/Gov ernment_debt, mises.org, shadowstats.com, gao.gov, MyGovCost.org, fms.treas.gov, usgovernmentspending.com, cia.gov, USDebtClock.org .

Appendices:

****** Appendix 1 ******

'Wars and the Lies That Start Them'

By David Redick

First published Mon. SEP 10, 2007   Wisconsin State Journal **www.madison.com**. a regional daily newspaper based in Madison, WI)

ALSO OCT.2, 2007 IN YORK NEWS TIMES, YORK, NE; **http://www.yorknewstimes.com/stories/100207/editorial_warlies .shtml**)

And, http://www.activistpost.com/2010/12/13-lies-abbreviated-history-of-us.html#more

****

Our presidents, and their complicit henchmen, have lied us into every war since the revolution in 1776.

Their real reasons have not been legal, constitutional, or politically acceptable, so they invent one or more false reasons that they can "sell " to the people.

Sadly, most people believe the lies, and proudly support them as "wars for defense". They can't imagine that our leaders would be so evil as to spend the lives of our troops to gain their hidden political and economic goals for Empire-USA.

The secret plan of Bush and his gang was to: 1) Take over all oil in the Greater Middle East (from the northern 'xxstans' to north Africa) so we don't have to share it with China and India, 2) Land for bases, and 3) Defend Israel at any cost. Control of oil was the hidden reason for the Balkans, Afghan, Libya, and Iraq (Mali?) invasions and occupations.

Iran is their next target.

The war drums are beating in Washington to justify bombing Iran, so this is a good time to consider whether our leaders are lying again. Here are the facts on how we got into a few major wars. Each one could be a book, so please forgive the brevity.

War of 1812

Lies: In 1812, Congress declared war on England based primarily on their kidnapping ("impressment") of our sailors at sea. **Truth:** To drive England out of North America and get southern land. The war started with our invasion of Canada, at Detroit. We burned their Parliament buildings in York (now Toronto), so they burned DC ! The 'Star Spangled Banner' was written a week later when British boats shelled Baltimore Harbor.

Mexican-American War

Lies: Fight to defend our Texas border with Mexico. **Truth**: We invaded to expand, and took the northern half of Mexico, now our entire Southwest region (to Sonoma, CA).

Civil War

Lies: A fight to end slavery and preserve the union. **Truth**: The South seceded due to economic abuse by the North. It was an invasion by the North, not a civil war! The Emancipation Dec. ended slavery only in Southern states.

Spanish-American War

Lies: Spain blew-up the U.S. battleship Maine in Cuba's Havana harbor. **Truth:** The accidental explosion was used to invade Cuba, steal Puerto Rico, annex Hawaii, and kill 200,000 locals to put a base in the Philippines.

World War I

Lies: Join Europe to "Make the World Safe for Democracy " **Truth:** Wilson was convinced to join by U.S. war-goods firms who wanted the U.S. to be one of the peace negotiators so they would be paid by England and

France. Thus, thousands of our troops died, and brought home the flu epidemic of 1918 that killed millions in the U.S.!

World War II

Lies: Defend the United States from unprovoked attacks by Japan. **Truth**: FDR wanted to prevent Germany from becoming a world power, so he poked Japan until he got an "incident." The war also suppressed Japanese growth. Thus, the USA emerged from WW2 as the #1 world power.

Korean War

Lies: Defend America. **Truth:** Truman and the generals wanted a reason to have troops in the Far East area of our Empire.

Vietnam War

Lies: Johnson said Vietnam attacked our ships in the Gulf of Tonkin.
Truth: The United States (and the Rockefellers) didn't want to lose control of the southeast Asia region, and its oil, to China.

Gulf War

Lies: To defend Kuwait from Iraq. **Truth:** Saddam was a threat to Israel, and we wanted his oil.

Balkans

Lies: Prevent Serb killing of Bosnians. **Truth:** Get the Chinese out of Eastern Europe and Caspian Sea areas so they couldn't get control of the oil.

Afghanistan

Lies: The Taliban were hiding Osama. **Truth:** To build a gas/oil pipeline from the northern Turkmenistan to a warm water port near Karachi.

Iraq Invasion

Lies: Stop use of WMDs, or bring democracy. **Truth:** Oil, defense of Israel, land for permanent bases and restore oil sales in the U. S. Dollar.

Possible Iran War

Lies: They almost have an atom bomb. **Truth:** Oil for the U.S., cut off oil to China, impose use of USD for oil sales, and defense of Israel.

Possible N. Korea War

 Their missile and bomb tests and threats are none of our business (short of stupid defense agreements) and we should ignore them.

We must fight the Politicians and Generals, and stop their plans for war against Iran, N. Korea (and all other wars for Empire!!)

****

******* **Appendix 2** *******

Links to Dave's Published Essays:

To save typing, just click on links at Part 8 in the left margin of my site Forward-USA.org; the whole list below is there, plus updates and additions.

'1. Government Structure and Conduct

a) 'The Phases of Empires' , Aug-2010 ; How empires rise and fall, and how five key characteristics vary for each Phase. http://www.activistpost.com/2010/08/phases-of-empire.html#more (same as Chapter 2 herein)

http://theburningplatform.com/blog/tag/dave-redick/

http://lewrockwell.com/orig12/redick1.1.1.html 20Dec2011

b) 'The Cost of Building and Operating Empire-USA', Aug-2010

How owning colonies/territories, or controlling other countries, damages the economics, civil rights, and morals of the Homeland. http://www.activistpost.com/2010/08/cost-of-building-and-operating-empire.html#more

c) 'How Governments Abuse Our Patriotism' Aug-2010

How governments promote 'Patriotism' and take advantage of it for their wars, and other abuses. http://www.activistpost.com/2010/08/how-governments-abuse-our-patriotism.html Aug-2010

d) '13 Lies: An Abbreviated History of U.S. Presidents Leading Us to War' Dec-2010

'Also named; 'Wars and the Lies that Start Them'. Discloses how all major US wars since the Revolution were started with Lies by Presidents. See text in Appendix 1.

e) 'The Role of 9/11 in Middle East Resource Control'   Jan-2011 ; How 9/11 was a pre-planned 'trigger' to justify the WOT and the invasions of Afghan and Iraq **http://www.activistpost.com/2011/01/role-of-9-11-in-middle-east-resource.html**

f) 'Save the USA by Restoring Government to its proper Role' Nov. 2, 2012 update of original April 22, 2011

USA governments at all levels have grown in power since our founding, and are causing great social and economic harm with their regulations, spending, and abuses. The USA is at a tipping point where spending reductions and legal reforms must be made or we will have a more severe economic crash than we have experienced since 2008. Included in Chapter 5 above. **http://www.activistpost.com/2011/04/save-usa-by-restoring-government-to-its.html#more**

2. Monetary Systems

a)   'Why Use Gold as Money?'   Dec-2010

The benefits of using a commodity as money, and why the market prefers gold **http://www.activistpost.com/2010/12/why-use-gold-as-money.html**

b)   'How to Abolish the Fed and Convert to Gold as Money'   Jan-2011

A six-step plan to convert the US to gold as money, allow private mints, and the benefits it would bring. http://www.activistpost.com/2011/01/how-to-abolish-fed-and-convert-to-gold.html#

c) 'The Impact of Fiat Money as the World's Reserve Currency'   Aug-2010

There is always a major currency that; 1. banks worldwide use as their reserves, and 2. is used for trade between countries, which since 1920 it has been primarily the US Dollar. After abrogating the Dollar's gold backing in 1971, the US started creating trillions of fiat paper notes - - monetary inflation - - to pay for its excessive imports (causing 'offshoring' of jobs), wars and other excesses. This excessive money creation can only be done by the issuer of the world's primary reserve currency.   http://www.activistpost.com/2010/09/impact-of-fiat-money-as-worlds-reserve.html#more

d) 'A Plan to Save the Euro with Gold'   Nov. 30, 2011

European 'leaders' are in a panic to save the Euro! I offer a plan that could be invoked by Euro issuing nations with no risk to current Euro owners because all existing Euro currency would immediately be backed by gold, so there would be no 'run' to dump them.
http://www.activistpost.com/2011/11/three-step-plan-to-save-euro-with-gold.html#more

 e) 'Convert the USA Monetary System to Gold'   Jan. 25, 2012
This essay shows a detailed plan to implement conversion from fake Fed Notes (FFN !) to 'gold-as-money' (all free market, with private mints, no Fed, redeemable paper notes, gold weight as the unit of account, etc.) and all the positive changes that go with it.
http://www.activistpost.com/2012/01/convert-usa-monetary-system-to-gold.html#more

f) 'Germany Should Quit the Euro and Use Gold As Money', Sep. 1, 2012

The fiat Euro (no gold 'backing') gave politicians and banks a way to create new money to feed excessive spending and debt. A further weakness was the hope (assumption?) that the larger nations (Germany and France) would bail out the sick nations and banks. This is like giving more heroin to an addict.
http://www.activistpost.com/2012/09/germany-should-quit-euro-and-use-gold.html#more

3. General Economic and Social Issues

a) 'How is Independent Thinking is Connected to Freedom and Prosperity'   Aug-2010 ; Explores the concept of Independent Thinking, where a person decides what to believe and do, rather than seeking the comfort of following the mainstream. http://www.activistpost.com/2010/08/how-is-independent-thinking-connected.html

b) ' How Excessive Spending, Taxation, and Controls are Destroying the US Economy' Jan-2011; How excessive spending, taxation, and controls by government for wars, welfare, entitlements, subsidies, etc., mostly financed by debt or fake money from our central bank, is wrecking our economy and morals.

http://www.activistpost.com/2011/01/how-excess-spending-taxation-and.html

c) 'How Free-Market Choices Can Solve Our Health Care Problems'   March 3, 2011 ; A plan to improve care and reduce costs by; a) getting the federal government out of health care funding and control, b) end the AMA pricing cartel, and c) bringing free-market competition and choice to health care.

http://www.activistpost.com/2011/03/how-free-market-choices-can-solve-our.html

d) 'Should Government Manage the Economy?' , March 15, 2011 ; The biggest divides in thinking as to the proper role of government are whether it should; 1. Manage the economy and monetary system, and be paternalistic in providing cheap or free social services, or 2. Just protect the rights of its citizens.

http://www.activistpost.com/2011/03/should-government-manage-economy.html#more

e) The U.S. Government and Consumers are Big Spenders Heading for a Crash , Jan. 5, 2015

Most U.S. citizens have been spoiled by the profits made from stock and real estate investments since 1990, and they see the 2008 crash as just a bump in the road. They are not aware that the hot economy was a bubble caused by excessive creation of new money (monetary inflation), and that a bigger crash is coming

http://www.activistpost.com/2015/01/the-us-government-and-consumers-are-big.html

****** **Appendix 3** ******

President Reagan sent this letter to Dave to support his campaign for Congress in CA Dis-1 (then from Petaluma, and up the coast to Oregon; about 500 mi.) in 1984'

"The White House
Washington
October 17, 1984

I am pleased to send my greetings to all those gathered to honor Dave Redick for his dedication to the principles of our party.
While nation proclaim their fear of the future, and issue predictions of gloom and doom, Dave Redick stands with those who look to the future with hope and confidence. We know that by rededicating ourselves to the values which made America great, we can ensure a bright and prosperous future for ourselves and our children. Dave has been an active participant in this struggle, and he has demonstrated both vision and an ability to get practical results. We need Dave Redick in Washington so that we can build on the progress that has been made in the past four years and ensure a bright future.

Nancy and I join with you in commending Dave for his many achievements and in wishing him every success this November.

(signed) Ronald Reagan "

A. Trump Cabinet Members as of March 9, 2017
(All require Senate confirmation)

1. Rex W. Tillerson, Secretary of State

The former president and chief executive of Exxon Mobil would oversee a department that has centered on alliance building and globalism, which Mr. Trump has said he would dismantle.

Mr. Tillerson was sharply questioned on his views on Russia, where he has had close business ties. He expressed reservations on climate change and said that he did not view it as the imminent national security threat that some others did.

2. Steven Mnuchin, Treasury Secretary

The former Goldman Sachs executive would be responsible for government borrowing in financial markets. He would also be involved in assisting with any rewrite of the tax code and carrying out or lifting financial sanctions against foreign enemies.

Democrats on the Senate Finance Committee pressed Mr. Mnuchin on his use of offshore tax havens, his initial failure to disclose almost $100 million in assets and charges that a company he ran was overly aggressive in foreclosing on homes.

3. James N. Mattis , Defense Secretary

The retired general would shape the fight against the Islamic State while overseeing a military that is struggling to put in place two Obama-era initiatives: integrating women into combat roles and allowing transgender people to serve openly.

General Mattis diverged from Mr. Trump on several issues during his hearing, striking a tougher stance on Russia and a more supportive one on NATO and saying that he supported the Iran nuclear agreement.

4. Jeff Sessions, Attorney General

The senator from Alabama supports strict immigration enforcement and measures tough on crime. He would be responsible for carrying out Mr. Trump's "law and order" platform and could change how civil rights laws are enforced.

During the first day of his hearing, Mr. Sessions said that the law "absolutely" prohibits waterboarding, and he offered no hints about a workaround to reinstate it. On the second day, testimony from Representative John Lewis, a Georgia Democrat and civil rights leader, highlighted the racial undertones of Mr. Sessions's nomination.

5. Ryan Zinke, Interior Secretary

The representative from Montana and onetime Navy SEAL commander would decide the fate of Obama-era rules that stop public land development; curb the exploration of oil, coal and gas; and promote wind and solar power on public lands.

When asked about climate change during his hearing, Mr. Zinke broke with Mr. Trump, saying that he did not believe it was a hoax.

6. Wilbur Ross, Commerce Secretary

The investor, whose fortune is estimated by Forbes at $2.9 billion, has said the United States must free itself from the "bondage" of "bad trade agreements," and has advocated threats to impose steep tariffs on China.

During his hearing, Mr. Ross said he would prioritize making sweeping changes to the North American Free Trade Agreement, one of Mr. Trump's campaign promises.

7. Tom Price, Health and Human Services Secretary

Price, a Republican representative from Georgia and an orthopedic surgeon, has led the opposition to the Affordable Care Act in Congress. In this role he would help Mr. Trump achieve one of his central campaign promises: namely the act's repeal and replacement.

Mr. Price said in his first hearing that repealing the Affordable Care Act would not leave millions without health insurance, but he gave few details about the administration's plans to replace the law. During his second hearing, he faced heated questioning over his trading of medical and pharmaceutical stocks.

8. Ben Carson, Secretary of Housing and Urban Development

The former neurosurgeon would oversee fair-housing laws, the development of affordable housing and access to mortgage insurance. He has stressed individual effort, not government programs, as the key to overcoming poverty.

During his hearing, Mr. Carson faced pointed questions about past remarks on the dangers of federal assistance. "Safety net programs are important," he said. "I would never advocate abolishing them without having an alternative for people to follow."

9. Elaine L. Chao, Transportation Secretary

Ms. Chao, who was labor secretary under President George W. Bush, would oversee Mr. Trump's campaign pledge to increase funding to rebuild America's transportation infrastructure.

Ms. Chao's nomination has faced little opposition from lawmakers. She spent most of her hearing promising to further study the issues she will oversee.

10. Rick Perry, Energy Secretary

The former Texas governor, who in 2011 proposed scrapping the Energy Department while he was seeking the Republican nomination for president, would be responsible for protecting and managing the nation's arsenal of nuclear weapons.

During his hearing, Mr. Perry said that he regretted suggesting that the Energy Deparment be abolished, and he reversed his previous comments denying human-caused climate change, saying, "I believe some of it is naturally occurring, but some of it is also caused by man-made activity."

11. Betsy DeVos, Education Secretary

The former chairwoman of the Michigan Republican Party and an activist for school choice would oversee a department that Mr. Trump has said he wants to drastically shrink by shifting responsibilities to state and local governments. READ MORE »

In her highly partisan hearing, Ms. DeVos was criticized by Democrats for wanting to "privatize" public education but praised by Republicans for her support of charter schools and vouchers.

12. David J. Shulkin, Secretary of Veterans Affairs

Mr. Trump has chosen Mr. Shulkin, the current under secretary for health at the agency. Mr. Trump has argued that the Obama administration neglected the country's veterans, and he has called improving their care a top priority.

13. John F. Kelly, Homeland Security Secretary

Trump makes good on his promises of widespread deportations and building a wall, the retired four-star Marine general will be responsible for carrying them out.

During his remarkably subdued hearing, General Kelly appeared to put concerns to rest over Mr. Trump's more contentious stances, like forcing Muslims to register with the federal government.

14. Mike Pompeo, C.I.A. Director

The representative from Kansas and former Army officer would have to decide whether to undo a new C.I.A. "modernization" plan, and how to proceed if Mr. Trump orders a resumption of harsh interrogation tactics for terrorism suspects.

Mr. Pompeo said that as C.I.A. director, he would pursue information about Russian interference into the American election. He said emphatically that he would not endorse torture, a reversal from past statements.

15. Nikki R. Haley, U.N. Ambassador

The governor of South Carolina would be the primary face of America to the world, representing the country's interests at the Security Council on a host of issues that include Middle East peace and nuclear proliferation.

Ms. Haley's nomination faced little opposition from lawmakers. During her hearing, she criticized the United Nations' relationship with Israel and said that Russia was guilty of war crimes in Syria.

16. Scott Pruitt, E.P.A. Administrator

The Oklahoma attorney general is a close ally of the fossil fuel industry and has taken on the E.P.A. directly in his current job. He would oversee an agency that the president has vowed to dismantle "in almost every form."

During his hearing, Mr. Pruitt said he disagreed with Mr. Trump's statement that climate change was a "hoax." He criticized federal environmental regulations, emphasizing a states-based approach.

17. Linda McMahon, Small Business Administration

The former chief executive of World Wrestling Entertainment would oversee an agency that guarantees loans for small businesses, helps them get government contracts and supports their interests on Capitol Hill.

Ms. McMahon, who was introduced and endorsed by two Democratic senators, faced a smooth hearing. She emphasized her entrepreneurial background and said she would fight against restrictive government regulations on businesses.

18. Mick Mulvaney, Director of the Office of Management and Budget

The conservative representative from South Carolina, a proponent of deep spending cuts, would help provide guidance with several of Mr. Trump's priorities, including a repeal of the Affordable Care Act, a tax overhaul and large investments in infrastructure.

During his hearing, Mr. Mulvaney promised to tackle wasteful government spending and the nation's debt. His toughest questioning came from Senator John McCain, Republican of Arizona, who asked Mr. Mulvaney about his record of voting for cuts to military spending.

19. Sonny Perdue, Agriculture Secretary

(Senate Hearing: T.B.D.)
The former governor of Georgia would run a department that oversees America's farming industry, inspects food quality and provides income-based food assistance. He would also have partial responsibility to carry out Mr. Trump's positions on trade.

20. R. Alexander Acosta, Labor Secretary

(Senate Hearing: T.B.D.)
Mr. Trump chose Mr. Acosta, a Florida law school dean and former assistant attorney general for civil rights, as his second labor secretary nominee, the day after Mr. Puzder withdrew from consideration. If confirmed, Mr. Acosta would be the only Hispanic in Mr. Trump's cabinet.

21. Dan Coats, Director of National Intelligence

(Senate Hearing: T.B.D.)
Mr. Coats served on the Senate intelligence and armed services committees while representing Indiana. Some in Mr. Trump's orbit believe that the job, overseeing the entire military and civilian intelligence apparatus, is superfluous.

The committee will likely confront Mr. Coats with Mr. Trump's own positions during his confirmation hearing.

22. Robert Lighthizer, U.S. Trade Representative

(Senate Hearing: T.B.D.)
The international lawyer served as a trade official under President Reagan. He role would include opposing new trade deals, trying to rewrite old ones and bolstering enforcement of trade agreements that Mr. Trump sees as unfair. »

23. Richard Grenell, Ambassador to NATO ; Grenell is a

veteran Republican foreign affairs spokesman. He is a

Trump supporter who served as a spokesman for John Bolton, former U.S. Ambassador to the United Nations, and several other GOP-appointed U.N. Ambassadors. An openly-gay Republican, Grenell would be one of the highest-ranking gay members of the Trump administration.

24. Jon Huntsman Jr., Ambassador to Russia. He is former Utah governor and Ambassador to China.

25. Justice Neil Gorsuch, Associate Justice of Supreme Court. While not on the Trump staff, he is a 'Constitutional Conservative', like Dave Redick, and it was considered a Trump victory that he was finally sworn in on April 10, 2017.

B. Senior Staff Members (Appointed: do not require Senate confirmation)

1. Reince Priebus, White House Chief of Staff

The departing chairman of the Republican National Committee is known as a dealmaker and is close with the House speaker, Paul D. Ryan. His role will be key in a White House run by Mr. Trump, who has no experience in making policy.

2. Stephen K. Bannon, Chief Strategist

Mr. Bannon is a right-wing media executive who has been criticized as representing racist views as the former head of Breitbart News. He was demoted from Trumps' inner-circle on Apr 10, 2017, but still partners" with Mr. Priebus, the Chief of Staff.

3. Jared Kushner, Senior adviser to the President:

A major developer in New York, Mr. Kushner is married to Mr. Trump's daughter Ivanka and has been a close adviser to the President. Mr. Kushner's appointment to the senior White House role could test anti-nepotism laws.

4. Thomas P. Bossert, Homeland Security Adviser

A top national security aide to President George W. Bush, Mr. Bossert now runs a risk management consulting firm and is a senior fellow at the Atlantic Council research institution. The position will be equal in status to the national security adviser.

5. Kellyanne Conway, Senior Counselor

Mr. Trump's campaign manager, confidante and spokeswoman, Ms. Conway also has a background in polling and may rely on these skills to keep tabs on public sentiment as she helps set the president's agenda.

6. Carl Icahn, Special Adviser on Regulatory Reform

The billionaire investor and famed "corporate raider" will oversee Mr. Trump's promised effort to unwind as many regulations on business as he can.

7. Donald F. McGahn II, White House Counsel

The Washington lawyer may have an unusually daunting job as the president's adviser on legal matters, given Mr. Trump's far-reaching business empire and potential conflicts of interest.

8. Peter Navarro, Director of Trade and Industrial Policy

The professor, who has been a staunch critic of current Chinese economic policies, is the only credentialed economist in Mr. Trump's inner circle. He will direct a new internal council overseeing White House trade and industrial policy.

9. Sean Spicer, Press Secretary and Special Assistant to the President.

Mr. Spicer was the longtime spokesman for the Republican National Committee and top aide to Mr. Priebus. Mr. Spicer will be the face of the White House, framing messaging, responding to stories of the day and briefing the press.

10. Lt. Gen. H.R. McMaster, National Security Adviser.

General McMaster is seen as one of the Army's leading intellectuals. As a commander, he was credited with demonstrating how a different counterterrorism strategy could defeat insurgents in Iraq. Replaces Gen. Flynn.

11. Hope Hicks, Director of Strategic Communications.

Ms. Hicks is one of the few people who worked for Donald Trump throughout the entire length of his presidential campaign. She served as Trump's press secretary throughout the campaign. She is 26, and has been described as his right-hand woman.

12. Ivanka Trump, the Presidents' daughter, is a Senior Advisor.

She is a successful business person, and is married to Jared Kushner (p. 173, #3).

13. Kevin Hasset, Chairman of the Council of Economic Advisers:

He was 'Director of Research for Domestic Policy' at the American Enterprise Institute (AEI.org). It is no longer a Cabinet position. Many AEI members are 'neocons' whose top priorities are war and defense of Israel.

14. Scott Gottlieb, Chm. 'Food and Drug Administration' (FDA) —

On March 10, 2017, the President appointed Gottlieb to chair the FDA. He is a pharmaceutical industry insider, and venture capitalist, who has served on the Boards of multiple pharmaceutical companies.

15. Erik Prince is a shadow consultant to Pres. Trump, and brother of Education Sec. Betsy DeVos (p.168). Both were big donors to his 2016 campaign. Prince is Chairman of Frontier Services Group **http://www.fsgroup.com/erik-prince.html**. They do supply and security to 'frontier' sites. He was Pres. of Blackwater Protection (**https://blackwaterprotection.com/**), a private security firm. They were hired by Pres. Bush to wage war in Iraq and killed many people, including civilians. The legality of this is under study.

16. Gary Cohn, Director of National Economic Council. Cohn was a top officer at Goldman-Sachs, and is reportedly on the short list to replace Reince Priebus as White House Chief of Staff. He is a 'globalist liberal.

17. (Other jobs); a) Jason Greenblatt, Chief Legal Officer, b) Keith Schiller, Dir. of Oval Office Operations (was Security Guard for Trump), and c) Omaras Monigault, Ass't to Pres. (was on 'Reality TV').

18.   (more coming?)

Xxxxxx (End) xxxx

Xxxxx (reserved) xxxxx

Glossary:

A. **Economics:** (Types, or 'Bodies of Thought')

1. 'Austrian School' of economic thought (Hayek, von Mises, Rothbard), emphasizes the spontaneous organizing power of free market pricing, decisions by individuals, gold as money, and little or no government management or stimulation of the economy.

2. Capitalism - An 'economic system' based on private ownership, free enterprise, and minimal regulation. It offers more than economic results. **It is a moral system** that depends on willing buyers and sellers within the rule of law, not coercion and control by others. It has been re-defined as a mean, self-centered, you're on your own, 'social system' by those who prefer Socialism (sharing by force, causing a more equal but lower standard of living for all). The U.S. now has 'Crony Capitalism', a damaging distortion where firms get favors from government (often in exchange for campaign donations!).

3. Communism: The government owns all housing, agriculture, industry and transportation (almost everything but the clothes on your back). The government tells you where to live, go to college (if any), and where to work.

4. Fascism allows private ownership of businesses, but there is extensive government control and preeminence.

5. 'Keynesian Theory' (started by J. M. Keynes in 1933; now used by Krugman, Samuelson, Stiglitz, Bernanke) depends on massive use of government fiscal (spending) and monetary policy (interest rates, money supply), in trying to create prosperity or avoid and end depressions. History and logic show the Keynes approach is unsustainable and never works for more than a year or two (longer if supported by natural resources; oil, timber, mining, etc.). Academic folks like it because it provides jobs and grants to them.

6. Monetarism: An approach identified with the 'Chicago School' of economics was led by the late Prof. Milton Friedman Ph.D. of the University of Chicago. It emphasizes management of the money supply by the Fed to control inflation and GDP growth. Most Monetarists dislike the gold standard as 'too inflexible' in changing the money supply. They are wrong because they ignore (or haven't thought of) how the purchasing power of gold increases with more demand. Thus, there is always 'enough'. They claim to like 'free markets', but also like the Fed; a conflict!

7. Socialism: Most of the means of production and trade (factories, railroads, etc) are owned by the government, which sets pricing, product types, etc. The government controls most wages, with an emphasis on 'fairness', need, and 'hours worked', rather than value of the service performed. High, and steeply progressive, taxes support a 'single-payer health system and pension plan

8. 'Supply-Side' : This emphasizes increasing the incentive to invest by reductions in; **a.** capital gains and income taxes (focusing on lower marginal rates), and **b.** regulation. These should be the first steps to revive a troubled economy because they have the lasting effect of stimulating action by producers and investors (on the 'supply', not 'consumer-demand', side) which increases jobs and the GDP. "Supply-Side' was originated by economists P. C. Roberts Ph.D., Robert Mundell Ph.D., and Arthur Laffer Ph.D., and politicians Pres. Ronald Reagan and Rep. Jack Kemp in the 1980s.

B. Free Market: A market which is free from government intervention (i.e. no regulation except to prevent force, theft and fraud; no subsidies; no monopoly **monetary system**; and no governmental monopolies). In a free market, property rights (ownership of goods and services) are voluntarily exchanged at a price arranged solely by the mutual consent of sellers and buyers, with no government control of pricing, creation of new firms, pay and benefits, hiring and firing, etc. The government's only role is to protect the rights of its citizens and legal visitors.

C. Gang Theft: This occurs when one group of people in some manner over-power another group, and forcibly take assets from them. Most people agree that it is immoral, and should be illegal, but oddly, most people (Liberals and Conservatives) believe it is OK to employ gang-theft-by-vote to tax, restrict, or control others (usually higher tax rates on 'the rich' or 'more privileged'; note that they already pay more per person even with a flat-rate tax!), via government power as the larger group sees fit. **This in fact describes an immoral government.**

D. Greed: An excessive desire for advantage or benefits that ends up hurting the seeker. Examples are: 1. investing in high-risk securities, and losing, 2. breaking laws and policy, and getting caught, or 3. working so hard that you hurt your health and family. This is not to be confused with 'Success', defined below. Liberals and Progressives often view them as the same, based on the false assumption that most 'successful' people are also greedy and have immoral or 'unearned' or 'luck' income. This helps them justify their 'tax the rich' schemes. (see 'Gang Theft' above)

E. **Honor:** A person gains honor by ethical, meritorious, principled, conduct, which may be performed even when his/her conduct is unknown to others.

F. Loyalty: 1. Faithful to lawful government, 2. True to any person to whom one owes fidelity,

G. Misconduct: 1. Corruption: Illegal acts, **2. Abuse:** Unethical, but not illegal

H. Neo-Conservative: Neoconservatism **(commonly shortened to** neocon**) is a political movement born in the United States during the 1960s among Democrats who became disenchanted with the party's domestic and especially foreign policy. Neoconservatives played a major role in promoting and planning the** 2003 invasion of Iraq **(which included defense of Israel).**[] **Prominent neoconservatives in the George W. Bush administration included** Paul Wolfowitz, John Bolton, Elliott Abrams, Richard Perle, **J. Gaffney, and** Paul Bremer. **Pres. George W. Bush listened closely to neoconservative advisers regarding foreign policy, especially the defense and growth (land, water, etc.) of Israel. There have been questions of their dual-loyalty (USA vs Israel), and which is first. Publications are Commentary and The Weekly Standard. Read more at; AIPAC.org,** https://en.wikipedia.org/wiki/Neoconservatism**, and P.C. Robert's Feb-2016;** http://www.paulcraigroberts.org/pages/books/the-**neoconservative-threat-to-world-order/** .

I. Political 'Establishment'**: The group of people who wield power to change the views and goals of politicians to serve their own interests, using money (campaign donations or secret bribes), political help, or threats of political damage.**

J. Principle: An underlying guide to thinking and action.A comprehensive and fundamental law, doctrine, or assumption. A rule, or code of conduct. "Principles are intended especially to guide our behavior in difficult circumstances. If they don't do so, then our proclaimed principles stand revealed as having been nothing but rhetoric in the worst sense of the word.", Robert Higgs, Independent.org. Principles can be refined over time, but not based on needs of the moment.

K. Sacrifice; Voluntary giving of some desirable thing in behalf of a higher, noble, claim

L. Statist: A **political viewpoint** that **sovereignty** is vested not in the **people** but in the national state, and that all individuals and associations exist only to enhance the power, the prestige, and the well-being of the state. The fascist concept of statism repudiates individualism and exalts the nation as an organic body headed by the Supreme Leader and nurtured by unity, force, and discipline (by Wikipedia). An example is Pres. Obama.

M. Success with Honor: The seeker achieves goals in a principled, productive, lawful, sustainable, and ethical way.

Xxxxx Reserved xxxxx

Biography of Dave Redick

Personal: Dave grew up with his two brothers in a middle class family near Detroit, MI. When he was 14, the family moved to an 80-acre general farm near Ann Arbor, Michigan. He has an honorable discharge from the U.S. Army Reserve.

Education and Business: Dave won a four-year tuition scholarship to the University of Michigan, based on grades, activities (Sr. Class President, sports), and need, and started in the fall of 1953. He completed his engineering degree in Feb., 1958. Upon graduation he worked as an aerospace engineer for 5 years (rocket engines and satellites) in California, and then started his career in telecom sales and management. In 1965 he earned an MBA in Economics from Santa Clara University in Santa Clara, CA, and after management positions in several other firms, in 1995 became VP Sales, then President, of a wireless engineering consulting firm **www.hntelecom.com**. He left in 2000 to be VP and cofounder of a Silicon Valley telecom startup 'Fiberstreet' (closed, see Google), and helped raise $6 million of venture capital. In 2005 he started 'Sustainable Energy Earth', an energy consulting firm.

Political: In 1978, Dave became concerned about economic and social damage caused by counterproductive government 'management'. He then read about and discussed this subject widely and became an activist for more cost-effective, and less abusive, government. He ran for Congress as a Libertarian in 1982 in District CA-1 (got 3% of vote), then returned to his Republican roots and ran in CA-1 again in 1984 with Reagan (got 38% with same issue positions!). He ran for State Legislature as a Republican in CA-24 in 2004, and in WI-77 in 2010. During the G. W. Bush administration, Dave became concerned about the Republican Party's departure from its core principles. In 2007 he was the Wisconsin contact for The Republican Liberty Caucus (see **www.WI.RLC.org** and **www.RLC.org**), which promotes the principles of limited government and free enterprise. In 2008 Dave founded the 'Forward USA Foundation' to promote better government. The website is **www.forward-usa.org**.

Index: Pages for topics in Glossary or book text headings are bold type

xxxxx End xxxxx